Bearing Fruit Without Ceasing

I0079186

McDougal & Associates
*Servants of Christ and Stewards of the
Mysteries of God*

Bearing Fruit Without Ceasing

By

Steven R. Murr

Published by:

McDougal & Associates
18896 Greenwell Springs Road
Greenwell Springs, LA 70739

www.thepublishedword.com

McDougal & Associates is an organization dedicated to the spreading the Gospel of the Lord Jesus Christ to as many people as possible in the shortest time possible.

ISBN: 978-1-950398-07-2

Printed in the U.S., the U.K. and Australia
For Worldwide Distribution

Dedication

I dedicate this book to you, the reader, and to all those believers in Jesus who are not satisfied with mediocrity. To you who hunger and thirst for more of Jesus, I present this biblical guide to progress. May you be filled, blessed and overwhelmed with the very presence of the only One Who really matters—JESUS.

Acknowledgements

First and foremost, my relationship with Jesus was, has been and still is the greatest and most important influence in my life. Writing a book is no easy task, but when the Holy Spirit inspires, it becomes easy. After thousands of hours of researching, praying, checking and double-checking the Word of God, this book was birthed in my spirit and written out.

Jesus brought certain people into my life who helped shape my way of thinking, people like Wallace Heflin Jr., Ruth Ward Heflin, Edith Heflin and George Slaughter, all connected with the Calvary Pentecostal Campground in Ashland, Virginia. They made a major difference in my life by introducing me to the dynamic and powerful presence and fellowship of the Holy Ghost.

Brothers and friends in Christ, like Steve Coffeen and Dr. Bill Dahlquist, connected with the Full Gospel Business Men's Fellowship, helped and influenced me to press forward into all that God had for me, by teaching me how to pray for people with their example.

People like Chester Smith and Jim Selpulvada shaped the way I moved in ministry, as I first copied their style and later developed my own.

Brothers in Christ, like the General Overseer of the Redeemed Christian Church of God, Dr. Enoch Adeboye, as well as Pastor Dr. Ajibike Akinkoye, encouraged me to continue a walk of holiness and faithfulness.

Others, like my instructors at Christ for the Nations Institute, Dr. Jack Hatcher and his wife Alta, poured into me both knowledge and experience.

Dr. Carroll Thompson also showed me, by his example, how to walk in the peace of God as a missionary or apostle to the nations.

John P. Turner, another missionary I met in this journey, encouraged me to keep the faith.

People like Pastors Steve and Gaye Vanzant of the Christian Center of Fort Worth showed me love and encouragement when mine ran low.

Judson Cornwall inspired me to continue writing as he counseled and prayed for me concerning my future in ministry.

Last, but certainly not least, my thanks are due to a true father in the faith: Pastor George M. Stover, Jr. of the Wellspring Church of All Nations in Las Vegas, Nevada. Pastor George has since gone on to

Glory and will be missed by all who knew him. He showed me the love I had not received from my own father. He encouraged me and inspired me more than anyone I know, to dig deep into the hidden treasures to be found in the Scriptures. I will forever remember the wonderful balance of mercy and truth he imparted into my life.

Contents

"Behold,
I
come
quickly!"

says the
Lord.

Introduction
(The Journey)

And they overcame him by the blood of the
Lamb, and by the word of their testimony; and
they loved not their lives unto the death.

Revelation 12:11

I was born into a Presbyterian family during the time my dad was in the U.S. Navy, and much of my childhood, therefore, was spent moving from place to place. I took my first breath on March 27, 1958 at Tripler Naval Hospital on the island of Oahu in Hawaii. At the time, Hawaii was still called the Territory of Hawaii. It didn't become a state until 1960. My family went from Honolulu to Florida, living in several other states along the way.

My sister DeAnne, was born May 7, 1960, and I became a big brother. It was an interesting childhood with all the usual conflicts between siblings.

Don't get me wrong. I love my sister and, in fact, she turned out to be the white sheep of the family.

We were raised in the Presbyterian Church because our mother was religious and made us go. I hated it, but, strangely enough, I later ended up being a Sunday school teacher in that denomination long before I ever had a "born-again" experience.

Growing up in a military family had its disadvantages. Because of moving from place to place, friendships were hard to forge. Forming friendships became even more difficult as I realized more and more that they would not last. As a result, I often found myself alone. This was why I started to talk to God.

I wasn't so sure that God actually heard anything I said, but I just kept talking to Him about everything. I firmly believed that He existed, but I didn't really know much about Him. My mother would pray for me often, and she always told me that God had a plan for my life. I didn't even pretend to understand what she was talking about. I just politely nodded my head.

A pivotal event that marked a change of direction in my life happened while my family was living in the countryside of South Texas, between Skidmore and Tynan. We were living in a house in the middle of a grain field. The event in question centered around the death of my great-grandmother, whom I called Nana. It was after Nana's death that I had my first real experience with God.

I had fond memories of Nana reading the Bible to me while I sat on her knee. Now I was twelve and she was gone. As a twelve-year-old boy, I understood almost nothing about death. I knew very little about talking to God except that you were supposed to pray in Jesus' name. I also knew that there was a Heaven and a Hell, but I was not sure about how you ended up in either place. I do remember that I thought that if you were good you would probably go to Heaven, and if you were bad you would definitely go to Hell.

Of course I know today that what I thought then is not really true. Many "good" people have died and gone straight to Hell. The righteousness of even what we would consider "a good man" is not nearly enough to earn entrance into Heaven. We must be cleansed from all sin by the blood of Jesus in order to make it in.

For us to avail ourselves of the opportunity to gain entrance into Heaven, we must first repent of sin and receive and trustingly rely upon the Christ, Jesus, and the blood that He shed on Calvary's tree.

He declared righteous all who trust in the payment for sin God offered through His Son. We cannot even add works to it in order to make Heaven. It is a work of the grace of God alone. If it did include works, man would have something to brag about.

I was greatly troubled about Nana's death and began to question the Lord concerning her salvation. I remembered that she had many times read the Bible to me. She had told me that Jesus loved me so very much and that He had died on the cross for me. I looked upon her with great affection, even though I really didn't know her all that well. I could tell, however, that she loved me.

After hearing of Nana's death, I began to think of eternal things. For three days, I went around doing very little except thinking of her and asking the Lord over and over the same question, "Where is she? In Jesus' name, where is she?" I was actually quite persistent in my asking, and I expected an answer.

If you have children, I am sure you can relate to this. Children don't seem to stop until you say yes or give in to their requests. Personally, I think we could all benefit by applying this concept to our prayer life. Speaking to God, considering that He hears us and praying persistently until we have our answer yields great results.

Introduction

Now, let's get back to my testimony. On the third day after Nana's death, I was doing what most healthy boys do—climbing a tree. After I had settled into the tree, sitting there in a sturdy fork, I once again asked the Lord that question, "Where is she?" While I was sitting there with the sun behind my back, the brightest Light I ever saw suddenly appeared before me. It was so bright I couldn't look at it. Waves of love coming from this light pounded upon me and went through me—wave after wave after wave.

I could make out what appeared to be the outline of a man in the midst of this light, and I knew it was Jesus. Then, the most beautiful voice I had ever heard spoke just three words. This voice that came forth had waves of its own, and they went through me like electricity. As I listened, along with an even greater intensity of love, I experienced what I can only describe as pure truth. What the voice said was, "She's with Me."

The light disappeared just as quickly as it had appeared, and as I continued to sit there in awe of what I had just experienced, I suddenly realized that the One by whom all things were made, the Lord of Hosts, the King of Kings, the Lord of Lords, the One whose glory spans the heavens, had just spoken to an insignificant little boy, and I became terrified.

I quickly climbed down out of that tree and ran to our house. As I burst in through the back door and began telling my mother what had just happened, she looked at me in utter amazement and shock. Years later, she told me that it was actually what she saw as I came through the door that day that shocked her. She said my face was covered with a light so bright that it was hard to look upon.

After that experience, I began talking to God more and more. I would walk down that dirt road in the middle of nowhere in South Texas, having long conversations with God and giving Him thanks for loving me and speaking to me. One thing I know for sure: when anyone has an encounter with God, it draws them to Him.

That experience drew me into a fellowship with God that I had never experienced before. I would sing and make up songs to Jesus and the Father. Looking back, I'm sure the Holy Ghost was helping me with it. It was a joyful time of fellowship with the Lord.

This lasted for a time ... until the family made a pilgrimage away from South Texas to Jacksonville, Florida. Then my fellowship with God quickly vanished, and I experienced a downward spiral.

Introduction

It started when I found myself in the middle of racial tensions and death threats as a young teenager. Before I got to Florida, I had never considered race to be an issue. Now it suddenly was.

My first girlfriend in high school was the daughter of a Baptist minister, and I really liked her. But feelings for each other didn't last long. Soon her father called my parents and asked them to get me to leave his daughter alone. She was receiving death threats, and so was I. Why? Because she didn't have the same skin color as I did.

I told my parents that this whole racial prejudice thing was pretty stupid, and they agreed. Nevertheless, I had to obey and not see my friend again, and in this way, I lost a wonderful friend because of the foolishness of many on both sides of the racial issue. Racial riots were taking place and violent conflicts were the news of the day in Southern Georgia and Northern Florida.

It was shortly after that sad episode that God suddenly got moved to the bottom of my list of priorities. Much more important to me at the time was acting tough, chasing girls, drinking alcohol and smoking cigarettes. These all took His place.

My life continued on that downward spiral until, in 1986, things had gotten so out of control that I decided to take my own life. I am ashamed to say that I had, by then, left my wife Jane for a younger woman and suddenly found myself alone with my worst enemy—me. I didn't tell anyone what I was thinking, but I made some serious plans to kill myself and end the misery I was in.

Then, through a series of bizarre circumstances, I met Jesus face to face and found myself on my knees in a hotel room. I found a Gideon Bible in that room and began to devour its life-giving pages.

I was in Las Vegas, Nevada, at the time, and my turnaround was so marked that I quickly began preaching the Gospel to anyone and everyone who would listen. Needless to say, I am leaving out some fairly powerful experiences that I had and perhaps I may include them at another time.

Through the gentle leading of the Holy Spirit, I next made an exodus from that place and went to Ashland, Virginia, to attend a Pentecostal campground there run by the Heflin family. While I was there, Jesus gloriously baptized me in the Holy Ghost at the hand of the late Brother George Slaughter. What a sweet-hearted man he was!

The camp was called Calvary Pentecostal Campground. It was overseen at that time by a true father in the faith, Reverend Wallace Heflin, Jr. He also pastored the principal church in Richmond, with his mother, Reverend Edith Heflin at his side, and his sister Ruth Heflin was a missionary living and working in Jerusalem. After more than sixty years of operation, that camp still goes on today. I stayed in the camp for two months and then returned to Nevada.

A side note here: am I the only one who has had the mind-set that the term *Holy Ghost* just sounds more powerfully Pentecostal and holy than *Holy Spirit*? We are pretty funny sometimes.

The atmosphere of both the church and the campground were charged with electric expectancy. Praise to God was fervent and joyous, with laughter, smiles, joy, dancing, sweating, and tears, as well as a deep sense of peace. The praise in each service would go on for close to forty-five minutes, much longer than in any traditional church. Dancing before the Lord and people falling down as the presence of God touched them was an ongoing thing.

In that atmosphere, miracles took place without the need for prayer. Lives were touched and hearts changed as the glory of God would come into the services. The prophetic also flowed freely and with order. There was both joy and reverential fear of God evident.

The dead were even raised in that place. I know of two people who died and were raised from the dead there. This was the atmosphere in which Jesus had gloriously baptized me in the Holy Ghost. What a privilege God had given me!

When I got back to Nevada, I went to my wife Jane and asked her forgiveness. I didn't expect that she would forgive me, but she did. I did not know it, but she had been born again while God was drawing me at the same time. Together we made a decision to serve God and follow Jesus wherever and whatever He led us to do. It is unfortunate, but Jane died a few years later from cancer. This really tested my faith, since I had prayed for others and cancer had disappeared. I had prayed for her too, but I saw no results. It broke my heart but only strengthened my resolve to serve God and tread down the enemy.

From 1991 to 1996, I was a member of the Full Gospel Business Men's Fellowship International, and served the Lord in the Las Vegas chapter as an officer. It was during my time with this fellowship that God began preparing me for my future in ministry. It was also during this time that I met my father in the Lord, Pastor George Stover. He has been the strongest positive influence in my life, and I am deeply grateful to God for him.

Introduction

It was also around this time that I began doing prison ministry in two different prisons, and this lasted about two years. One of the prison ministries was through WECAN, and the other was through FGBMFI. To God belongs all the glory and to Him belongs all the praise for all the good things that have been done, are now being done and will be accomplished in my life.

Years later, another pastor, Steve Vanzant, who lives in Fort Worth, Texas, became another strong positive influence in my life. Both of these blessed men of God are near and dear to my heart. It has also been my privilege and honor to meet and stand with many other wonderful men and women of God in organizations like the Full Gospel Businessmen's Fellowship International, Business Men's Fellowship, USA, Full Gospel Fellowship of Churches and Missions, Redeemed Christian Church of God, Christ for the Nations Institute, Calvary Pentecostal Tabernacle, Fort Worth Christian Center and Wellspring Church of All Nations—to name just a few. All of these have contributed greatly to shaping my future in Christ.

The Lord has privileged me to see with my own eyes transformations that took place after I spoke His Word that was given to me. I have seen with my own eyes the blind seeing, the lame leaping and running like a deer and the deaf hearing after the Lord had me to pray and led me about how to do it.

Through the years, I have stood in amazement as bones were snapped back into their proper places. I have watched with eyes of confidence and also with amazement at times as God illustrated His Word. I watched as a little baby near death because of sickness and high fever (probably from bad water) was miraculously touched and healed. The baby's skin had changed from grey to a healthy pink, as the fever instantly disappeared.

So many times I have seen the faithfulness of the Lord and His Word, as I cast out demons by the unction of the Holy Ghost and the people were set free, even as others praised and enjoyed the glory of the Lord.

Once an older woman who was stooped over came up to me and asked for prayer. She had been hit by a car, her body had healed in that position, and the spine had calcified. She spoke to me in Indonesian, but my translator told me, "She says, 'If God can heal those others, He can heal me too.' "

I said "I can't do anything, but Jesus can. Let's see what He does!"

She fell to the floor as so many had and, as she began to stir, someone helped her to a chair. While she was sitting there, rather of slouched over in the chair, she began to speak very loudly, even more loudly than me (and I had a microphone). I stopped and asked the translator what she was saying. He told me, "She's telling everyone that things are moving around in her back right now!" When that lady stood up to leave at the end of that meeting, she was standing upright. The Lord is a miracle-worker, and His Word never fails!

I have danced in the glory and felt so light that I thought I was going to fly. I have seen visions, too many to number. I have seen the angels of the Lord in services and watched as they danced along with the people. I have watched demons leave when the glory of the Lord fell upon the people. I have heard the voice of the Lord as He declared from the heavenlies, "Come up! Come up! Ascend on the wings of praise!"

I have seen and heard these things in that realm of glory where anything (and I mean anything) is possible. The glory is that atmosphere of Heaven that comes into a meeting when praise and then worship establishes the very presence of the Lord of Hosts. I believe in miracles because I believe in the Miracle Worker! Praise the Lord Jesus Christ!

Over the years, I have served Him, doing various types of ministry. I have discovered that the best ministry of all is that of ministering to God in praise and in prayer. Learning to be the best at praising Jesus, worshipping the God of Abraham, Isaac and Jacob is my heart's desire.

I don't play any musical instruments, and I have no special musical skills. I just love to sing praises to Jesus! I have a simple desire to be nearer and nearer to Him and to praise Him more and more. My desire is to worship the King of Kings and the Lord of Lords. I pray that is your desire too, to become a worshipper of God!

I was working on this book in Dipolog City, within the Province of Zamboanga Del Norte on the island of Mindanao in the Philippines. My wife, Lorena, and I were entrusted by God with our daughter Deborah born in 2010. My daughter Gabriella born in 1997 did not want to remain in the Philippines and is currently going to school in the U.S. while living with my mother in Fort Worth, Texas.

Lorena and I live by faith, trusting God to supply our food, rent and all other needs. We have never gone hungry during the years I have been here. Though our support has been seemingly almost non-existent at times, we are still here and God is with us.

A few years ago, before Deborah could ever speak, a young girl named J-nissi, one of the members of a praise team, was wrestling with God about doing something He asked of them. J-nissi didn't know if she could do what God was asking. Deborah, who could speak no language except baby talk, toddled over to her and spoke to her in perfect Cebuano, "I will be with you. I will help you." J-nissi was in awe because she knew it had to be God talking to her through Deborah.

Last year, while playing, Deborah fell and hit her head. A big knot quickly swelled up on her head (close to the size of a golf ball) and began turning purple. Deborah was crying, and people gathered around her to look at the bleeding gash on her forehead.

Lorena called for me, and I came and prayed, as others agreed, for Deborah to be healed. When I removed my hand, there was no evidence of a gash, no swelling, and the purple was gone. We wiped the blood off of Deborah's forehead to find no evidence at all of a fall. People were amazed! That is my Jesus! Now, anytime someone needs prayer, Deborah either tells me to pray or she prays for them herself. God is awesome!

A local pastor asked me to go to Sicayab Hospital to pray for one of his members, an older woman, who had suffered a stroke. She was unable to move, could not talk and could not even open her eyes. I prayed for her, expecting an immediate result, but I didn't see any change at that moment.

As I got ready to leave the hospital, I was talking to God, asking Him why an anointing was released with no immediate result. No answer came, so I simply gave it to God and said to Him, "Your will be accomplished."

As I was going out, a young brother called for me, asking me to come back. I did. It turned out that another woman who was visiting in the same room had seen me praying, and now she was asking if I could pray for her sixteen-year-old daughter who was hospitalized in that same room. They had brought her in because she had gone completely blind.

The doctors had told them that she would never see again, that the cells at the back of her eyes (which are responsible for the reflection of light) were completely dead and useless. I prayed, and by the anointing in the name of Jesus, commanded her to open her eyes and look at me. She opened her eyes, and, amazingly, she could see! Jesus is always amazing to me!

The next day the woman who had suffered the stroke opened her eyes and began speaking and moving. God is so awesome!

Introduction

About a year later the girl who had received her sight that day suddenly fell into a coma and was diagnosed with encephalitis. This is a virus that attacks the nerve centers of the brain. Apparently, it sometimes leaves its victims permanently paralyzed to varying degrees. The mother now contacted me, asking for my help. I went to them and prayed for her daughter once again. A few hours later she came out of the coma.

I went to visit and pray for the young girl again after she was admitted to the hospital. Before I prayed, I was told that she was unable to speak or move. But, after prayer, she was both speaking and moving. God is so good!

A few months ago, I was asked to participate in an evangelistic crusade and to speak on healing as it is included in our salvation. I did this, and many were healed of various illnesses and infirmities: lungs cleared, lumps disappeared, pain was instantly gone, eyesight cleared, etc. Jesus Christ is the same yesterday, today and forever! May God be praised! In my thinking, this marks the beginning of the long-awaited harvest, signaling the soon return of Him for Whom my heart longs, my beloved Jesus! Praise our risen King!

God has truly blessed me. Sometimes I feel like the Forrest Gump of Christianity. I have been so fortunate to meet so many blessed and power-filled servants of the Lord and have witnessed as well as participated in powerful healings and miracles. I am completely cognitive of the fact that it has absolutely nothing to do with any great qualification on my part! I am so grateful to God that the Gospel we preach is not a powerless Gospel. He fills us with life and power!

This book has been written and re-written many times over during the last nineteen years. My first writing was a booklet entitled *Soaring with the Eagles*. I lost track of that booklet, although a copy of it can be found in the Library of Congress. Fortunately, from that time to now, my understanding has progressively deepened. To my chagrin, I have discovered my errors. I am grateful for the Spirit of Wisdom and Revelation in the knowledge of His Word. It has been quite a journey. Although I have tripped over my own feet many times, I thank God for His faithfulness. He has always been there, cheering me on to victory in every area of my life and ministry.

My prayer for you is that this book benefits you greatly. If you are blessed in some small way by the message of it, I will have reached my goal.

—Steven Murr

Chapter 1

Are You Meditating on God's Word?

The heart of the wise teacheth his mouth, and addeth learning to his lips. Pleasant words are as an honeycomb, sweet to the soul, and health to the bones. Proverbs 16:23-24

It is my understanding that the best place to start with anything is at the beginning, so that's what I am doing. About twenty-five years ago now, I came across a small booklet written by an unknown man from an obscure place. I really was not looking for anything in particular, but when I found this little book, I began reading it and became fascinated with the concept that the writer was attempting to convey. What he said inspired me so much that I decided to investigate and either prove the man completely wrong with scripture or prove him right.

I did word studies, word searches, application studies and asked questions of anyone who seemed to have knowledge of this concept. It was not until 1994 that I began to put the concept, as I understood it at the time, into print. The writing of *Soaring with the Eagles* was the beginning.

The reason I spent so much time on researching these writings was that it was not a popular concept at the time, and I wanted to make very certain that I was not buying into a lie. Moreover, I had not been inspired to put anything into print until that time.

During my investigation, the word *meditate* came to my attention. I had understood the meaning of *meditate* to be simply "to think upon." Now I looked up this word *meditate* in *Strong's Exhaustive Concordance*. The Hebrew and Chaldee Dictionary in the back of the *Strong's Concordance* gave a definition that included much more than I had ever realized. The word *meditate*, it said, *hagah* in Hebrew, means "to murmur, to ponder, imagine, mutter, speak, study, talk and utter." So my idea or understanding of the word had been very incomplete.

The words *speak, talk* and *utter*, as well as *murmur* and *mutter* began to ring in my spirit with insistence. All my life I had been taught to study and read quietly. Now, I could see where I had missed something. Since it was clear that I had missed it, I decided to look more deeply into this subject. A scripture from Joshua seemed to make a convincing case for the benefits of speaking the Word of God out loud:

> *This Book of the Law shall not depart out of your mouth, but you shall **meditate** on it day and night, that you may observe and do according to all that is written in it. For then you shall make your way prosperous, and then you shall deal wisely and have good success.*
> Joshua 1:8

Again, this word translated *meditate* was *hagah*, and now that I knew what *hagah* meant, I read it again. *"You shall **[murmur, ponder, imagine, mutter, speak, study, talk and utter]** on it day and night."*

After seeing this, I went on to look deeper into the Word of God and found that this understanding was consistent with several other biblical references:

> *Blessed is the man that walketh not in the council of the ungodly, nor sitteth in the seat of the scornful. But his delight is in the law of the LORD; and in his law doth he **meditate** day and night.*
> Psalm 1:1-2

There is was again! *"In His law doth he [murmur, ponder, imagine, mutter, speak, study, talk and utter] day and night."* In another verse, I read:

> *My eyes anticipate the night watches and I am awake before the cry of the watchman, that I may meditate on your Word.* Psalm 119:148

What was it really saying? *"I am awake before the cry of the watchman, that I may [murmur, ponder, imagine, mutter, speak, study, talk and utter] on Your Word."*

Wow! It was getting all the more convincing!

Well, that was fine for the word *meditate,* but was there another witness? I read in Proverbs:

> *Listen (consent and submit) to the words of the wise, and apply your mind to my knowledge; for it will be pleasant if you keep them in your mind [believing them]; your lips will be accustomed to [confessing] them.* Proverbs 22:17-18, AMPC

My lips will be accustomed to confessing what? *"The words of the wise"* can be understood to be the Word of God! Can we agree that Jesus is the Word of God?

Are You Meditating on God's Word?

And he was clothed with a vesture dipped in blood: and his name is called The Word of God.
Revelation 19:13

Can we agree that Jesus is our wisdom?

But of him are ye in Christ Jesus, who of God is made unto us wisdom, and righteousness, and sanctification, and redemption.
1 Corinthians 1:30

Next, I saw that *confession* or *speaking* was what confirmed or brought to fulness our salvation. Look at what the Bible tells us in Romans:

Because if you acknowledge and confess with your lips that Jesus is LORD and in your heart believe (adhere to, trust in and rely on the truth) that God raised Him from the dead, you will be saved. For with the heart a person believes (adheres to, trusts in and relies on Christ) and so is justified (declared righteous, acceptable to God),and with the mouth he confesses (declares openly and speaks out freely his faith) and confirms [his] salvation.
Romans 10:9-10, AMPC

This scripture sets a precedent that can be used to consistently justify confession or speaking. Moreover, throughout the Scriptures we can find justification for repeating what the Word of God says about us. Look, for instance, at what the Lord says in Deuteronomy 6:

> *Hear, O Israel; the LORD our God is one LORD [the only LORD]. And you shall love the LORD your God with all your [mind and] heart and with your entire being and with all your might. And these words which I am commanding you this day shall be [first] in your [own] minds and hearts; [then] You shall whet and sharpen them so as to make them penetrate and teach and impress them diligently upon the [minds and] hearts of your children, and shall talk of them when you sit in your house and when you walk by the way, and when you lie down and when you rise up.* Deuteronomy 6:4-7, AMPC

These scriptures make it very clear that it is the Word of God that we are to be rehearsing to ourselves, to our children and to our neighbors. *"When you walk by the way"* is, most likely, the time we would be talking about the Word of God to neighbors and to people we are just meeting. When you include *"when you lie down and when you rise up,"* it seems to include most of our time.

It is also important to note here that although this set of verses in the Scriptures is referring to the Law, a precedent is being set to speak the Word.

A side note about meditation: This point must be brought out and emphatically declared. Meditation, according to the Word of God, is NOT clearing your mind of all things and focusing on nothingness. Focusing on anything other than the Word of God, as Philippians 4 instructs us, isn't what the Word of God is speaking of concerning meditation. The reason I say this is so that we are not mimicking New-Age, Kabbalah and Buddhist techniques such as "emptying yourself," which is pure foolishness that can lead to demonic influences.

When someone empties himself or herself, they become an empty vessel that any breeze of any spirit can enter. The Holy Spirit will not normally come uninvited. Focusing our mind on the Word of God helps us to have a healthy and stable mind. Let's be careful to focus on that which the Lord has instructed us:

For the rest, brethren, whatever is true, whatever is worthy of reverence and is honorable and seemly, whatever is just, whatever is pure, whatever is lovely and lovable, whatever is kind and winsome and gracious, if there is any virtue and excellence, if there is anything worthy of praise, think on and weigh and take account of these things [fix your minds on them].

Philippians 4:8, AMPC

So, quiet study and pondering the Word of God is a primary part of the meaning of the word *meditate*. But we are missing it if that is all that we are doing in our time of meditation. I believe this aspect of meditation was observed widely across China and is most beneficial, along with muttering or speaking the Word of God aloud.

The reason I say this is that before the 1960s almost all Bibles in China were hand-written. House churches were fortunate to have even one Bible. Each family would get their turn with a part of that Bible. Often pages were torn out, hand-copied and passed around. After they finished copying each page, it was returned and they would take another one. As the pages were meticulously copied and each word taken in and pondered, I imagine they would read slowly and aloud in the process in order to check their work of copying. This fulfilled the meaning of meditation described in the Scriptures and, as a result, the faith level of many Chinese became much higher, and that opened the way for them to experience miracles.

The meditation I am talking about here is what brings revelation knowledge of God's Word, and revelation knowledge of God's Word is the material that makes up the building blocks that produce and cause faith to bloom. Meditation, when mixed with the fellowship of the Holy Spirit, can make you unstoppable.

You can speak the pure Word of God to your neighbor, *"when you walk by the way,"* and you, too, may find yourself experiencing miracles!

Now I began to see more and more in the Scriptures concerning *speaking*. The importance of what we say and the content of what we say became increasingly apparent:

> *A man's [moral] self shall be filled with the fruit of his mouth; and with the consequence of his words he must be satisfied [whether good or evil]. Death or life are in the power of the*

tongue, and they who indulge in it shall eat the fruit of it [for death or life].

Proverbs 18:20-21, AMPC

What did Solomon say the words that we speak can do? Wow! We eat the fruit of our own words. This means that we will eat the fruit of speaking God's Word.

The downside is this: we also eat the fruit of negative confessions! Reading that scripture made me want to go about with tape over my mouth, just in case. This passage of scripture told me that I had better start watching what I was saying. It also told me that those words I spoke ought to be His rightly-divided Word.

Chapter 2

Are You Hearing the Word?

The lips of the wise disperse knowledge [sifting it as chaff from the grain]; not so the mind of the self-confident and foolish.

Proverbs 15:7, AMPC

It seemed like the more I thought about words, the more I saw both the benefit and the cost to us. One day I said, "Wait a minute! When you speak, you hear what you are saying! Hhmmmm!" In the book of Mark, Jesus had something to say about what you hear:

And He said to them, be careful what you are hearing. The measure [of thought and study] you give [to the truth you hear] will be the

39

*measure [of virtue and knowledge] that
comes back to you—and more [besides] will
be given to you who hear.*

Mark 4:24, AMPC

As is so clearly stated by Jesus, we get what
we give or sow (plant). The more I studied and
thought about the Word of God, the more knowledge I had and the better my character became.

Another amazing effect of hearing the Word
of God is, of course, obvious; faith is produced:

*So then faith cometh by hearing, and hearing
by the word of God.* Romans 10:17

So we can have a better character by hearing
the Word of God, and we were feeding ourselves
faith food at the same time. So, it's all in how
much time I am willing to invest in the Word of
God.

"Do you mean that I am responsible for my own
growth?" some might ask. Yes and no. Yes, because God has to have something in us to quicken
or make alive. No, because only the Lord can
make us grow after the Word of God is planted

and watered. It is God who gives the increase:

> *So then neither he who plants is anything, nor*
> *he who waters, but God who gives the increase.*
>
> 1 Corinthians 3:7

If God's Word cannot be found in us, how can we say that *He* is in us? Didn't Jesus say in John?

> *If you live in Me [abide vitally united to Me]*
> *and My words remain in you and continue to*
> *live in your hearts, ask whatever you will, and*
> *it shall be done for you.* John 15:7, AMPC

Jesus also told us that if His Word was not in us, we would hate Him:

> *If the Son therefore shall make you free, ye shall*
> *be free indeed. I know that ye are Abraham's*
> *seed; but ye seek to kill me, because my word*
> *hath no place in you. I speak that which I have*
> *seen with my Father; and ye do that which ye*
> *have seen with your father.* John 8:36-38

> *If the world hate you, ye know that it hated Me*
> *before it hated you. If ye were of the world, the*

41

world would love his own: but because ye are not of the world, but I have chosen you out of the world, therefore the world hateth you.   John 15:18-19

So we must have God's Word in us.

Jesus said that if we hate Him, we hate the Father also:

He that hateth Me hateth My Father also.
John 15:23

An important note: I believe that if all of us, as Christians, truly love one another as the Lord would have us to love, we might find that raising folks from the dead and other miracles would be a natural consequence. It says, in Galatians 5, that faith works *"by love"*:

For in Jesus Christ neither circumcision availeth any thing, nor uncircumcision; but faith which worketh by love.   Galatians 5:6

So let's not kid ourselves. None of us love as much as the Lord wants us to.

Now that we have all of this information, we are left with a choice. Will we follow the precedent of "confession" in our Christian walk, or will we choose to disregard what is plainly explained in the Bible? As James put it:

> *Wherefore, my beloved brethren, let every man be swift to hear, slow to speak, slow to wrath: For the wrath of man worketh not the righteousness of God. Wherefore lay apart all filthiness and superfluity of naughtiness, and receive with meekness the engrafted word, which is able to save your souls.*
>
> *But be ye doers of the word, and not hearers only, deceiving your own selves. For if any be a hearer of the word, and not a doer, he is like unto a man beholding his natural face in a glass: for he beholdeth himself, and goeth his way, and straightway forgetteth what manner of man he was. But whoso looketh into the perfect law of liberty, and continueth therein, he being not a forgetful hearer, but a doer of the work, this man shall be blessed in his deed. If any man among you seem to be religious, and bridleth not his tongue, but deceiveth his own heart, this man's religion is vain.* James 1:19-26

It is so very important that we learn to control our speech and speak in agreement with the Word of

God. A bridle is used on horses to direct them. According to *Webster's Dictionary*, a bridle is "used to restrain, guide or govern; to check, curb or control."

Here are a few more references on the importance of bridling our tongues:

Keep thy tongue from evil, and thy lips from speaking guile. Psalm 34:13

And my tongue shall speak of thy righteousness and of thy praise all the day long. Psalm 35:28

My tongue shall speak of thy word: for all thy commandments are righteousness.
Psalm 119:172

The tongue of the just is as choice silver: the heart of the wicked is little worth.
Proverbs 10:20

A wholesome tongue is a tree of life: but perverseness therein is a breach in the spirit.
Proverbs 15:4

Whoso keepeth his mouth and his tongue keepeth his soul from troubles. Proverbs 21:23

Are You Hearing the Word?

For in many things we offend all. If any man offend not in word, the same is a perfect man, and able also to bridle the whole body.

James 3:2

For he that will love life, and see good days, let him refrain his tongue from evil, and his lips that they speak no guile.   1 Peter 3:10

If you still have not decided to speak out or confess the Word of God, perhaps we should go back to what Jesus told us in Mark 4:

And He said to them, be careful what you are hearing. The measure [of thought and study] you give [to the truth you hear] will be the measure [of virtue and knowledge] that comes back to you—and more [besides] will be given to you who hear.   Mark 4:24, AMPC

In this verse, Jesus said *"be careful what you are hearing."* What are we listening to and how much of it is the Word of God? How many of us are content to sit back and watch television? It is not only important to govern what we are hearing, but also what we are seeing.

Bearing Fruit Without Ceasing

*I will set no wicked thing before mine eyes: I
hate the work of them that turn aside; it shall
not cleave to me.* Psalm 101:3

Even if it is Christian television, it may not always be the pure Word of God. I love Christian
television, but it should never be a substitute for
meditating on the Word of God or fellowshipping
with other believers. Although we are in this world,
let us not be connected with those things that bring
impurity:

*I pray not that thou shouldest take them out of
the world, but that thou shouldest keep them
from the evil. They are not of the world, even
as I am not of the world.* John 17:15-16

*Wherefore come out from among them, and be
ye separate, saith the Lord, and touch not the
unclean thing; and I will receive you.*
2 Corinthians 6:17

Didn't God tell us to *"meditate"* (murmur, ponder,
imagine, mutter, speak study, talk and utter) on His
Word day and night? In this verse in Mark 4, Jesus
pointed out that the measure we give will be the

measure that comes back to us and more also for those who hear.

Mark 4 isn't the only witness. Let's see what the Word is speaking to us in Galatians 6:

Be not deceived; God is not mocked: for whatso-ever a man soweth, that shall he also reap. For he that soweth to his flesh shall of the flesh reap corruption; but he that soweth to the Spirit shall of the Spirit reap life everlasting.

Galatians 6:7-8

If we study and speak the Word of God and invite the Holy Ghost to help us understand, our reward is a refined character, as we yield to the Word and humble ourselves. Why? Because the Word of God cleans our mind and cuts away at our flesh. The Word of God, as it is quickened in us, is very alive and very, very real.

Jesus said in John 15:

Now ye are clean through the word which I have spoken unto you. John 15:3

The Word of God lives!

For the Word of God that God speaks is alive and full of power [making it active, operating, energizing, and effective]; it is sharper than any two-edged sword, penetrating to the dividing line of the breath of life (soul) and [the immortal] spirit, and of joints and marrow [of the deepest parts of our nature], exposing and sifting and analyzing and judging the very thoughts and purposes of the heart. And not a creature exists that is concealed from His sight, but all things are open and exposed, naked and defenseless to the eyes of Him with Whom we have to do.   Hebrews 4:12-13, AMPC

In John 6, Jesus brought out the fact that His words are alive:

It is the spirit that quickeneth; the flesh profiteth nothing: the words that I speak unto you, they are spirit, and they are life.   John 6:63

Our words can be spirit and life too, as we yield our lives completely into the hand of the Master. Do you believe that?

Let me ask you a question. Concerning the words that Jesus spoke, who gave Him those words? Wasn't it the Holy Spirit? Who breathed the written Word of God? Wasn't it also the Holy Spirit? The words Jesus has spoken to us, and He is still speaking to us. His words are spirit and life. The words of God are only written words on a page until His Spirit quickens them to us.

When God created all things, He gave the first example of seedtime and harvest. He planted the seed of His Word by speaking words of Spirit and life, which brought forth the harvest of creation. All of His Words are Spirit and life:

> *In the beginning God created the heaven and the earth. And the earth was without form, and void; and darkness was upon the face of the deep. And the Spirit of God moved upon the face of the waters. And God said, Let there be light: and there was light. And God saw the light, that it was good: and God divided the light from the darkness. And God called the light Day, and the darkness he called Night. And the evening and the morning were the first day.* Genesis 1:1-5

I have heard it said that the Holy Spirit hovered over the earth, the Father willed creation, and the

Son spoke it into existence. God, Who is Spirit, planted the seed of His Word by speaking:

> *God is a Spirit: and they that worship him must worship him in spirit and in truth.* John 4:24

In His Parable of the Sower, Jesus called the seed the Word of God:

> *Now the parable is this: The seed is the word of God.* Luke 8:11

When the Holy Spirit is leading us to speak God's Word, it can be just as powerful as if it came from the lips of Jesus the Anointed One Himself! This is yet another reason that it is so important to be led by the Holy Ghost in what we do and what we say.

As we draw closer and closer to Jesus, He leads us into revelation understanding of His Word. Depending on the Holy Ghost to lead us in this relationship, we enter into an adventurous journey. The Holy Ghost repeats to us what is spoken at God's very throne:

> *Howbeit when he, the Spirit of truth, is come, he will guide you into all truth: for he shall not*

Are You Hearing the Word?

speak of himself; but whatsoever he shall hear, that shall he speak: and he will shew you things to come. John 16:13

Take the journey! Hear His Word!

Chapter 3

Are You Speaking the Word?

Right and just lips are the delight of a king, and he loves him who speaks what is right.
                                        Proverbs 16:13, AMPC

Another discovery of the application of the confession of God's Word came about while I was doing a study on Creation and how the Holy Spirit was involved. During this study, I revisited scriptures pertaining to Creation. The same basic conclusions can be drawn from them. The Holy Spirit hovered over the face of the waters, the Father willed Creation, and the Word spoke it into being. As Jesus spoke it, the Holy Spirit performed the Word:

In the beginning God (prepared, formed, fashioned) and created the heavens and the earth.

Are You Speaking the Word?

The earth was without form and an empty waste, and darkness was upon the face of the very great deep. The Spirit of God was moving, (hovering, brooding) over the face of the waters. And God said, Let there be light; and there was light. Genesis 1:1-3, AMPC

I was thinking about this, and then I thought about the Father's will in our lives as Christians. Knowing that there is so much this subject covers—such as redemption, adoption, empowering for service and authority—I changed my thoughts to speaking the will of God.

The will of God can be found in the Word of God. If I speak the will of God (His Word) for my life, then I see it! The Holy Spirit performs it!

Let me repeat that! The Holy Spirit performs the Word of God that I speak! That is the pattern. Remember, the Word of God must be taken in the context in which it was written.

Unbelief is the first thing that springs forth in the soul when the conclusion we reach is so bold. Such a conclusion, however, comes as we take all the scriptures together and in the context or setting for each scriptural reference. I checked it and rechecked it.

Was this conclusion in line with the Scriptures? Were there any passages that proved it? My conclusions were Yes and Yes! Many scriptures are in line with this conclusion. If you look for this simple point as you search the Scriptures, you will find more passages that confirm it. Let me give you just a few examples that I quickly found:

> *So let us seize and hold fast and retain without wavering the hope we cherish and confess, and our acknowledgment of it, for He Who promised is reliable (sure) and faithful to His word.*
> Hebrews 10:23, AMPC

> *It is the spirit that quickeneth; the flesh profiteth nothing: the words that I speak unto you, they are spirit, and they are life.* John 6:63

> *Then said the LORD to me, You have seen well, for I am alert and active, watching over My word to perform it.* Jeremiah 1:12, AMPC

> *For as the rain and snow come down from the heavens, and return not there again, but water the earth and make it bring forth and sprout, that it may give seed to the sower and bread to*

Are You Speaking the Word?

the eater, so shall My word be that goes forth out of My mouth; it shall not return to me void—without producing any effect, useless—but it shall accomplish that which I please and purpose, and it shall prosper in the thing for which I sent it.   Isaiah 55:10-11, AMPC

Now, let me ask you a question. To whom was the Word of God sent? Did God not send His Word to you and me?

He sent his word, and healed them, and delivered them from their destructions.

Psalm 107:20

And he was clothed with a vesture dipped in blood: and his name is called The Word of God.

Revelation 19:13

For God sent not his Son into the world to condemn the world; but that the world through him might be saved.   John 3:17

If the Word of God is in us, what is meant here by *"it shall prosper in the thing for which I sent it"*? Since God's Word was sent to us, how is His Word returned to Him? Bingo! There was my answer. We speak it!

Now I want to stress a point here: nowhere have I said anything about us *being* God. The Word of God shows that we are *like* God, not that we *are* God. His Word shows that we, as Christians, are *in* Him and this is an act of His grace. This is often misunderstood when this subject is brought up.

Because we are seated with Christ in heavenly places, all that applies to Christ applies to us (except, of course, the most important part). What is that? He is in charge! It is as we are led by His Spirit and His Word that we take dominion, because it is His will!

In God's Kingdom, there is only one Lord, and His name is Jesus. Because we are part of His Body, when the enemy looks at us, He sees Jesus. That is ... if we have put our flesh under subjection to our spirit. In effect and as a result of this, we do not question the Scriptures, but rather we establish and fulfill them as truth.

Look at what the Bible tells us in Deuteronomy 6:

Hear, O Israel: The Lord our God is one Lord.
Deuteronomy 6:4

Are You Speaking the Word?

When Jesus came into the world, He not only gave us redemption, adoption, empowering for service and authority; He also showed us what we were to do and how we were to do it. While being tempted by the devil in the wilderness, Jesus did not tell the devil what a good person He was or all the good works He had done. Instead, Jesus spoke the Word of the Lord in its proper application. We can see by His example that we also are to speak the Word of the Lord in a correct application.

By Jesus' example and because of the fact that He is the living Word, the defeat of Satan was made manifest. We must have that same Word coming from our lips. We should not depend upon preachers and ministers to speak the Word of God for us. We must speak it for ourselves.

Revelation 12:11 tells us that it is by the blood of the Lamb and the word of our testimony that we overcome the devil:

> *And they have overcome (conquered) him by means of the blood of the Lamb and by the utterance of their testimony, for they did not love and cling to life even when faced with death [holding their lives cheap till they had to die for their witnessing].*
>
> Revelation 12:11, AMPC

Our testimony is our confession! In *Strong's Exhaustive Concordance*, the word *testimony* is listed as #3141. In the Greek dictionary in the back of the concordance, it is shown to mean "evidence given (either judicial or general) by record, report, testimony, witness." This term *judicial* indicates "a record that can be taken to court," and let me tell you this: God's written holy Word is that kind of evidence!

The term *general* refers to other evidence, probably the kind not well documented, such as personal testimony. So we have covered two types of testimony as illustrated in *Strong's:* the spoken Word of God and the spoken personal word, and both are a testimony. One is from the Lord and it becomes part of us, and the other is our personal experience with the Lord.

It is easy to get stuck on this point. I've known people who rejected any form of personal testimony in connection with this verse. I've also known some who almost totally overlooked the written Word aspect of their testimony. In doing this, they are missing a key ingredient:

> *And I fell at his feet to worship him. And he said unto me, See thou do it not: I am thy fellowservant, and of thy brethren that have the testimony of Jesus: worship God: for the testimony of Jesus is the spirit of prophecy.* Revelation 19:10

Chapter 4

Are You Sowing the Word?

From the fruit of his words a man shall be satisfied with good, and the work of a man's hands shall come back to him.

Proverbs 12:14, AMPC

Hear ye therefore the parable of the sower. When any one heareth the word of the kingdom, and understandeth it not, then cometh the wicked one, and catcheth away that which was sown in his heart. This is he which received seed by the way side. But he that received the seed into stony places, the same is he that heareth the word, and anon with joy receiveth it; yet hath he not root in himself, but dureth for a while: for when tribulation or persecution ariseth because of the word, by and by he is offended. He also that received seed among the thorns is he that heareth the word; and the care of this world, and the deceitfulness of riches, choke the word, and he becometh unfruitful. But he that received seed into the good ground is he that heareth the word, and understandeth it; which also beareth fruit, and bringeth forth, some an hundredfold, some sixty, some thirty.

Matthew 13:18-23

Here in the Parable of the Sower, Jesus told us (in verse 19), that the seed to be sown is the Word of the Kingdom. The Amplified Bible capitalizes *Word* in this verse.

In telling the same parable, Mark 4:14 says, *"The sower sows the Word."* Luke also makes the meaning abundantly clear:

Now the parable is this: The seed is the word of God. Luke 8:11

Now that we know that the seed is the Word of God, what would the ground be? Let's look at a few scriptures in order to see:

Are You Sowing the Word?

Upon the land of my people shall come up thorns and briers ... .   Isaiah 32:13

And all nations shall call you blessed: for ye shall be a delightsome land, saith the LORD of hosts.   Malachi 3:12

You [Judah] shall no more be termed Forsaken, nor shall your land be called Desolate any more. But you shall be called Hephzibah [My delight is in her], and your land be called Beulah [married]; for the LORD delights in you, and your land shall be married [owned and protected by the LORD].   Isaiah 62:4, AMPC

For as the earth bringeth forth her bud, and as the garden causeth the things that are sown in it to spring forth; so the LORD God will cause righteousness and praise to spring forth before all the nations.   Isaiah 61:11

And the LORD God formed man of the dust of the ground, and breathed into his nostrils the breath of life; and man became a living being.   Genesis 2:7

Bearing Fruit Without Ceasing

We can safely say, from these scriptures we have looked at, that the seed is the Word of God, and the ground is the people. We will come back to this point later. Now, however, let's look at what Jesus told Nicodemus in John 3:

> *Jesus answered and said unto him, Verily, verily, I say unto thee, Except a man be born again, he cannot see the kingdom of God.*
> *Nicodemus saith unto him, How can a man be born when he is old? Can he enter the second time into his mother's womb, and be born?*
> *Jesus answered, Verily, verily, I say unto thee, Except a man be born of water and of the Spirit, he cannot enter into the kingdom of God. That which is born of the flesh is flesh; and that which is born of the Spirit is spirit. Marvel not that I said unto thee, Ye must be born again. The wind bloweth where it listeth, and thou hearest the sound thereof, but canst not tell whence it cometh, and whither it goeth: so is every one that is born of the Spirit.*
> *Nicodemus answered and said unto him How can these things be?*
> *Jesus answered and said unto him, Art thou a master of Israel, and knowest not these things?*

Are You Sowing the Word?

Verily, verily, I say unto thee, We speak that we do know, and testify that we have seen; and ye receive not our witness. If I have told you earthly things, and ye believe not, how shall ye believe, if I tell you of heavenly things?

John 3:3-12

Referring to what He had just said to Nicodemus in verse 3 and verses 5 to 8, Jesus told Nicodemus (and us), *"If I have told you earthly things ..."* When I saw that, I said to myself, "Wait a minute! Verse 5 talks of being born of water and of the Spirit, and verse 7 says *"ye must be born again."*

Water is related to the Word in Ephesians:

That he might sanctify and cleanse it with the washing of water by the word.

Ephesians 5:26

At first, my mind just didn't want to accept that being born of water and of the Spirit, which is being born again, started as an earthly thing, and yet there it was right before me. How could I deny it?

Then it occurred to me that this was referring to an occurrence or event that takes place on Earth, although the water and the Spirit came from Heaven.

Since verses 3, 5, 7 and 8 were referred to as an earthly thing, couldn't this in some way relate to seed being sown in the earth, as found in Matthew chapter 13? Yes, of course. Thus, being "born again" would be the fruit or product of seed that was sown and then sprang up.

The seed of the Word is sown through preaching:

> *For there are three that bear record in heaven, the Father, the Word, and the Holy Ghost: and these three are one. And there are three that bear witness in earth, the Spirit, and the water, and the blood: and these three agree in one.*   1 John 5:7-8

To be born of water and of the Spirit, trusting in the blood Jesus shed on Calvary's tree, could be compared to a plant sprouting in the earth. We can easily see that the Parable of the Sower in Matthew 13 also illustrates to us the various conditions of our own soil. In addition to this, we can see that once we are "born again," we have become an earthen vessel that contains a heavenly treasure.

Look at 2 Corinthians 4:

> *However, we possess this precious treasure [the divine Light of the Gospel] in [frail, human]*

Are You Sowing the Word?

vessels of earth, that the grandeur and exceed-
ing greatness of the power may be shown to be
of God and not from ourselves.

2 Corinthians 4:7, AMPC

All of us want to believe that we are good ground
and that we will yield one hundred times as much as
is sown. After all, it has to be all those other people
that Jesus was referring to who are rocky and thorny
ground, not me, right? All the while, the other people
are thinking the same about us. To them, we are
those other people. We need to be sober and realistic
in our self-appraisal.

Paul wrote:

For by the grace (unmerited favor of God) given
to me I warn everyone among you not to esti-
mate and think of himself more highly than he
ought [not to have an exaggerated opinion of
his own importance], but to rate his ability with
sober judgment, each according to the degree of
faith apportioned by God to him.

Romans 12:3, AMPC

Please don't misunderstand me. We must be bal-
anced. The focus of this book is the value of the

spoken Word of God in our life. In order for this to be effective, we must yield ourselves to the work that the Lord desires to do in us by His holy written Word, as it is quickened to us and in us by His Spirit. We must be humble and yet filled with faith, and that is only produced from God's Word through the Holy Ghost.

We must be holy in our attitudes and actions so that an apparent difference between us and an unbeliever is quite noticeable. For this to be true, love must be a dominant factor in our character:

> *And therefore the LORD [earnestly] waits [expecting, looking, and longing] to be gracious to you; and therefore He lifts Himself up, that He may have mercy on you and show lovingkindness to you. For the LORD is a God of justice. Blessed (happy, fortunate, to be envied) are all those who [earnestly] wait for Him, who expect and look and long for Him [for His victory, His favor, His love, His peace, His joy, and His matchless, unbroken companionship]! O people who dwell in Zion at Jerusalem, you will weep no more. He will surely be gracious to you at the sound of your cry; when He hears it, He will answer you. And though the LORD*

Are You Sowing the Word?

gives you the bread of adversity and the water of affliction, yet your Teacher will not hide Himself any more, but your eyes will constantly behold your Teacher. And your ears will hear a word behind you, saying, This is the way; walk in it, when you turn to the right hand and when you turn to the left. Then you will defile your molten images plated with gold; you will cast them away as a filthy bloodstained cloth, and you will say to them, Be gone! Then will He give you rain for the seed with which you sow the soil, and bread grain from the produce of the ground, and it will be rich and plentiful. In that day your cattle will feed in large pastures.

Isaiah 30:18-23, AMPC

Chapter 5

What Kind of Ground Are You?

He who loves purity and the pure in heart, and who is gracious in speech, will for the grace of his lips have the king for his friend.

Proverbs 22:11, AMPC

And he spake many things unto them in parables, saying, Behold, a sower went forth to sow; and when he sowed, some seeds fell by the way side, and the fowls came and devoured them up: some fell upon stony places, where they had not much earth: and forthwith they sprung up, because they had no deepness of earth: and when the sun was up, they were scorched; and because they had no root, they withered away. And some fell among thorns; and the thorns sprung up, and choked them: but other fell into

What Kind of Ground Are You?

good ground, and brought forth fruit, some an hundredfold, some sixtyfold, some thirtyfold. Who hath ears to hear, let him hear.

Matthew 13:3-9

If you want to discover what type of ground you are (or someone else is), just listen to the words that come out of your/their mouth. Out of the abundance of the heart, the mouth speaks. You will know a tree by its fruit:

A good man out of the good treasure of his heart bringeth forth that which is good; and an evil man out of the evil treasure of his heart bringeth forth that which is evil: for of the abundance of the heart his mouth speaketh. Luke 6:45

Either make the tree good, and his fruit good; or else make the tree corrupt, and his fruit corrupt: for the tree is known by his fruit.

Matthew 12:33

It is when the heat is turned up on gold, as it is melted, that the impurities come to the surface. In the same way, when the heat is turned up in the life of someone who is a Christian, our hidden problems come to the surface. This doesn't happen to hurt us, but rather to show us our need to put our flesh under. This "heat" can come from trials or tribulations, but also comes as God prepares us to "hold" more of His anointing in our lives:

> *That the trial of your faith, being much more precious than of gold that perisheth, though it be tried with fire, might be found unto praise and honour and glory at the appearing of Jesus Christ.*   1 Peter 1:7

Our "ground" can be tilled and rocks and stones removed. Our mountains can be leveled. It is when we humble ourselves and invite the Holy Ghost to change us that we will see results.

The Parable of the Sower in Matthew 13 that we have been examining has included seed and ground. The different types of ground have not yet been discussed in any detail, so we will attempt to do that in this chapter. As stated, there are four basic types of ground. Jesus named them as "way side," "rocky," "thorny" and "good."

"Way side" ground is usually quite hard or resistant. You see this type of ground on a road or path. The surface of this ground is so solid that if water pours onto it, it will run off or puddle because of the great difficulty it has trying to soak in. You've seen this haven't you?

Can this phenomenon be seen in some of us? You know what I mean. Those of us who at one time or another have passed on a blessing, but never really changed our way of doing or thinking on a matter. A good example of it might be something like this: You hear a great sermon. It's very challenging to your lifestyle. You tell your neighbor about the sermon. But you don't change your own lifestyle, and you find a justification for why you don't need to change.

"Oh, that other guy really needed to hear that one!" you tell yourself. It didn't apply to you. With this type of ground, the seed just sits there on the surface, or it blows off, or the birds come and get it. Birds love this kind of ground. You can tell that because they spend so much time there.

If a person is this type of ground, you might say that the message was sent, but it wasn't mixed with faith because their eyes seemed to be veiled. This kind of person seems to be hard of hearing. We can only be rid of that veil by humbling ourselves and truly believing and trusting in Jesus to give us eyes to see and ears to hear His Word.

Paul wrote:

In fact, their minds were grown hard and cal-loused [they had become dull and had lost the power of understanding]; for until this present day, when the Old Testament (the old covenant) is being read, that same veil still lies [on their hearts], not being lifted [to reveal] that in Christ it is made void and done away. Yes, down to this [very] day whenever Moses is read, a veil lies upon their minds and hearts. But whenever a person turns [in repentance] to the Lord, the veil is stripped off and taken away.

2 Corinthians 3:14-16, AMPC

"Rocky" ground is that type of ground that has a thin layer of loose dirt on top but with rocks or stones beneath it. I once worked for a man who was probably the nicest guy I'd ever met. He would purchase or have me purchase very expensive flower seeds by the pound, and then he told me to cast them over the side of a certain hill.

The hill was very steep, and it had a lot of rocks on it. Because the man had me do this several times, it was not an inexpensive endeavor. To this day the flowers still don't grow in that place like he wanted them to grow. Seeds don't grow well in stony ground.

What Kind of Ground Are You?

The seed of the Word of God has a much higher price, and yet at times in my past I have considered it to be cheap. Have you? Anyway, as I was thinking about this type of ground my thoughts turned to John the Baptist:

> *As it is written in the book of the words of Isaiah the prophet, The voice of one crying in the wilderness [shouting in the desert]: Prepare the way of the Lord, make His beaten paths straight. Every valley and ravine shall be filled up, and every mountain and hill shall be leveled; and the crooked places shall be made straight, and the rough roads shall be made smooth.*
>
> Luke 3:4-5, AMPC

You may ask me what this has to do with "rocky" ground. Let's take a closer look. When ground is prepared for planting, one of the first requirements is that the ground be broken up. It is also necessary that the place to be planted be leveled as much as is possible. The reason for this is so that when the rain comes all of the seed will be evenly watered, giving the whole field a chance to bring forth the desired product from the seed planted.

Ground that is resistant to the breaking of the plow is often "rocky" ground. Spiritually speaking, this kind of ground could be easily referred to as proud ground. Pride, in my opinion, is what is referred to in this passage. Pride is the outer covering of most strongholds in the lives of people. Pride can be found as a reason for every type of sin.

A common expression you may have heard that illustrates this point goes something like "a proud heart is a hard heart." Often someone with pride is very easily offended:

> *A brother offended is harder to be won than a strong city: and their contentions are like the bars of a castle.* Proverbs 18:19

If a person is "rocky" ground and a little trouble comes his or her way, this person will probably get very angry or get their feelings hurt. Perhaps the Light begins to shine on areas you don't want to face or the Light shines so bright that you run away. Then, you might fall into sin again and even blame God:

> *The foolishness of man subverts his way [ruins his affairs]; then his heart is resentful and frets against the LORD.* Proverbs 19:3, AMPC

What Kind of Ground Are You?

Strongholds of darkness are the "rocks" in any ground. Let's destroy them by humbling ourselves to the Word of God.

With another look at Luke 3:3-4, we can see that mountains and hills are mentioned. If you know anything about land, you should know that mountains and hills are full of rocks. This also indicates pride that needs to be leveled. Again I say, let's humble ourselves that we might receive the Word of God that is able to save our souls:

> *Understand [this], my beloved brethren. Let every man be quick to hear [a ready listener], slow to speak, slow to take offense and to get angry. For man's anger does not promote the righteousness God [wishes and requires]. So get rid of all uncleanness and the rampant outgrowth of wickedness, and in a humble (gentle, modest) spirit receive and welcome the Word which implanted and rooted [in your hearts] contains the power to save your souls.*
> James 1:19-21, AMPC

"Thorny" ground is that ground that just gets "too busy" to focus on what Jesus would have us to do. "Thorny" ground is also that ground concerned with the cares of this world or the "need" to make money. Often, folks have fooled themselves into thinking that they have the right focus. Unfortunately, the reality is that they have their priorities out of order.

This ground may even have a concern for the things pertaining to the Lord, but not enough of a concern to pursue those things. This person could be described as someone who is rooted in God, but the focus of their attention over a period of time has become less and less God and more and more the world. This most likely did not happen overnight. It might have started by missing an occasional Sunday at church. The fire dies a little more each time. Perhaps they never repented and had the real experience of being born again. Perhaps, God put them in charge of a project, but because of their schedule they justified themselves out of it.

Is that you? Time may have long passed since the last time this person witnessed to anyone about Jesus. Perhaps you were filled with the Holy Spirit long ago. Maybe the only experience that you can talk about having with the Lord was way back before television was invented. If so, get up, shake off the dust and praise the Lord. Stir up the gift that is in you! It didn't go away! Jesus said He would never leave us or forsake us.

What Kind of Ground Are You?

According to a seventy-three-year-old evangelist from Pennsylvania who pastored for some forty-two years, the following story of the frog in the pan has been around since the early 1950s. I don't know where the story came from or I would give credit where credit is due. It goes like this:

If you take a frog and put it in a pan of boiling water, it will jump out fast, but if you put it in the pan and turn the heat up slowly, it will just stay right there until it's too late. Well, it's not too late for you! Get out of the pan! Rise up above your circumstances to the plan that God has for you. Make a change in your priorities. Put God first. Put the welfare of your fellow Christians first and prove it with your deeds.

Talk is cheap. Be generous and give your all to the Lord. Rise up in Him and let the glory of the Lord shine through you:

> *Arise shine; for thy light is come, and the glory of the LORD is risen upon thee. For, behold, the darkness shall cover the earth, and gross darkness the people: but the LORD shall arise upon thee, and his glory shall be seen upon thee.* Isaiah 60:1-2

Worldliness cannot be tolerated or accepted in any form in a born-again, Holy Spirit-filled, child of the Lord of Hosts. We need to be an example to the world, not a stumblingblock to a possible believer. Again I say, we must humble ourselves and keep our fallow ground broken before Him:

> *For thus says the* LORD *to the men of Judah and to Jerusalem: Break up your ground left uncultivated for a season, so that you may not sow among thorns. Circumcise yourselves to the* LORD *and take away the foreskins of your hearts, you men of Judah and inhabitants of Jerusalem, lest my wrath go forth like fire [consuming all that gets in its way] and burn so that no one can quench it because of the evil of your doings.*
>
> Jeremiah 4:3-4, AMPC

Note: *"the foreskin of your hearts"* indicates anything or any habit or way of doing things that can make your heart sick or infected. This refers to sin. Look at what Jesus says about a heart with two devotions:

> *No servant is able to serve two masters; for either he will hate the one and love the other, or he will stand by and be devoted to the one and despise the other. You cannot serve God and*

What Kind of Ground Are You?

mammon (riches or anything in which you trust and on which you rely). Luke 16:13, AMPC

Now, again, please don't misunderstand me here. It is fine to have lots of money — as long as the money doesn't have you! Let's serve God with a pure heart and a clear conscience by putting away every idol we may have in our lives. Let's put away the luxury of leading our own lives and let Jesus lead us.

If you know the Lord, you will also know that it is not always convenient to do what the Lord of Hosts wants you to do. Put the Lord in charge of your finances and focus on loving Him. If you hesitate to give when He prompts you, money has become too important to you. Get your priorities right, and give as freely as He has given to you. That money isn't yours anyway. We are just stewards of what we have. So, let us be good stewards:

> *And seek not ye what ye shall eat, or what ye shall drink, neither be ye of doubtful mind. For all these things do the nations of the world seek after: and your Father knoweth that ye have need of these things. But rather seek ye the kingdom of God: and all these things shall be added unto you.*   Luke 12:29-31

"Good" ground is that ground all of us want to be. It is that kind of ground that receives correction with a "thank you" in humility. This kind of ground is a delight to the heart of the King. We plant in this ground, and what we plant there grows and becomes well rooted.

This kind of soil has been thoroughly plowed and is level, preventing imbalances in understanding. The stones or strongholds surrounded by pride have been removed. All the weeds have been removed, along with their roots. There are no thorns because our focus of attention is correct. This ground remains broken up through humility and prayer, in order that the Righteous Seed may have His Way in the earth.

The whole purpose and reason for this ground is to feed, nourish and fully accommodate the Righteous Seed. May we all be found to be "good" ground! Let us start now by rooting out the "thorns" and casting the "rocks" away:

> *Sow for yourselves according to righteousness (uprightness and right standing with God); reap according to mercy and loving-kindness. Break up your uncultivated ground, for it is time to seek the LORD, to inquire for and of*

What Kind of Ground Are You?

Him, and to require His favor, till He comes and teaches you righteousness and rains His righteous gift of salvation upon you.

Hosea 10:12, AMPC

You and I know that when seed sprouts it produces more seed, and that sprouts and produces more seed, and so on and so on. The desired result is a flourishing harvest of fruit with righteousness.

I once heard a pastor say from the pulpit of his church, "You can count the seeds in an apple, but you cannot count the apples in one seed." I ask you please, please let the Word of God have its way in you. Give His seed time to germinate. Water it with more of His Word and praises. God is so good to us. Let us walk holy before Him.

As has been illustrated thus far in this book, we are the ground, and the Word of God is the righteous seed. We have also been shown that it is the Word of God spoken that casts the seed to the earth. This lays further "groundwork," so to speak, for making confessions of the Word of God out loud. The fruit, the leaves of healing, the aspect of being His garden and the majesty of kingly authority all come from the engrafted Word of God thriving in us through a dynamic personal relationship with the Lord Jesus

Christ. As has been said, let's plant it, water it and have the patience to receive the harvest from it.

Don't forget to pray for others that they, too, may have their fallow ground broken up and become receptive to the Righteous Seed:

> *Happy and fortunate are you who cast your seed upon all waters [when the river overflows its banks; for the seed will sink into the mud and when the waters subside, the plant will spring up; you will find it after many days and reap an abundant harvest], you who safely send forth the ox and the donkey [to range freely].*
>
> Isaiah 32:20, AMPC

Chapter 6

Are You Abiding in the Word?

Abide in me, and I in you. As the branch cannot bear fruit of itself, except it abide in the vine; no more can ye, except ye abide in me. John 15:4

I would be remiss if I did not speak to you about abiding in the Word of God. To abide in a place is to live there. *Webster* defines the word *abide* as "remain, to continue, to be firm and immovable to be, or exist, to continue to dwell, rest, stand firm." *Vines* says "to abide under (*hupo*, under), signifies 'to remain in a place instead of leaving it, to stay behind.' " Two verses in Isaiah indicate that we are part of the vineyard of God:

He shall cause them that come of Jacob to take root: Israel shall blossom and bud, and fill the face of the world with fruit.   Isaiah 27:6

Bearing Fruit Without Ceasing

For the vineyard of the LORD of hosts is the house of Israel, and the men of Judah his pleasant plant: ... .   Isaiah 5:7

We were grafted into the Vine through the grace of God and through faith:

For if the firstfruit is holy, the lump is also holy; and if the root is holy, so are the branches. And if some of the branches were broken off, and you, being a wild olive tree, were grafted in among them, and with them became a partaker of the root and fatness of the olive tree.
                                        Romans 11:16-17

Abiding in the Word of God implies that we are constantly looking at the Word of God while keeping it before our eyes:

The statutes of the LORD are right, rejoicing the heart: the commandment of the LORD is pure, enlightening the eyes.   Psalm 19:8

My son, let not them depart from thine eyes: keep sound wisdom and discretion.
                                        Proverbs 3:21

Are You Abiding in the Word?

*Let them not depart from thine eyes; keep them
in the midst of thine heart.* Proverbs 4:21

*Let thine eyes look right on, and let thine eyelids
look straight before thee.* Proverbs 4:25

Abiding in Jesus also implies that we do not place
anything wicked before our eyes:

*I will set nothing wicked before my eyes; I hate
the work of those who fall away; it shall not
cling to me.* Psalm 101:3

Jesus stressed the importance of abiding in Him.
He is the Word of God! It is that vital relationship
with Jesus that gives us life and all that is important
in it:

*I am the true vine, and my Father is the hus-
bandman. Every branch in me that beareth not
fruit he taketh away: and every branch that
beareth fruit, he purgeth it, that it may bring
forth more fruit. Now ye are clean through the
word which I have spoken unto you.*
*Abide in me, and I in you. As the branch cannot
bear fruit of itself, except it abide in the vine;*

*no more can ye, except ye abide in me. I am
the vine, ye are the branches: he that abideth
in me, and I in him, the same bringeth forth
much fruit: for without me ye can do nothing.
If a man abide not in me, he is cast forth as a
branch, and is withered; and men gather them,
and cast them into the fire, and they are burned.
If ye abide in me, and my words abide in you,
ye shall ask what ye will, and it shall be done
unto you. Herein is my Father glorified, that
ye bear much fruit; so shall ye be my disciples.*

John 15:1-8

Now, let's step back for a moment. In order to
abide in Christ, we must first be born from above
and have Jesus living in our heart by faith. This relationship is born and grows out of the grace God
gives us. Abiding in Christ indicates a close and
intimate relationship with Him. This relationship
cannot be superficial in any way; otherwise it is
religious fantasy.

The natural consequence of being joined with
Jesus is our love for Him, and that is proven by our
obedience to Him. He is the Author of salvation for
them that obey Him:

Are You Abiding in the Word?

And being made perfect, he became the author
of eternal salvation unto all them that obey him.
Hebrews 5:9

The natural consequence of not abiding in Jesus is that our spiritual life dries up and dies out. With this comes all manner of sin and, eventually, death:

If a man abide not in me, he is cast forth as a
branch, and is withered; and men gather them,
and cast them into the fire, and they are burned.
John 15:6

I gave an example of abiding in Jesus to a beautiful group of Christian folks by using the behavior of my youngest daughter Deborah to illustrate. When I ask Deborah to do something for me or to stop doing something and she obeys me, she is abiding in my word or instruction. Later, without me being present, my word will speak to her. Obeying Jesus is at the center of abiding in Him.

As we humble ourselves in obedience to His Word and spend time filling ourselves with the bread of God (His Word), we are cleansed, renewed and made whole. When we consistently walk in obedience to His Word, that Word finds place in us. As we are doing this, our love will grow more and more for the object of our affections—Jesus.

As we lie willingly and happily in the arms of the Beloved, we receive comfort, and we are pruned. With each stroke of the Sword of His Word, we cast away the nature of the flesh, and our love for Him is renewed and grows deeper. Suddenly, what we thought was so important is no longer nearly as important. He is all that matters!

Obedience to God's Word comes more quickly and naturally to us as we spend more time with Him in prayer and praise, and our character becomes so much like Jesus that spending time with Him becomes seemingly necessary for our survival. If you have trouble seeing your relationship with Jesus as between two lovers, then you need to get over it. Look past the natural and see it for what it is in the Spirit.

This is NOT about flesh and blood. This is a marriage of the Spirit. The desire to be in God's presence is much like being lovesick. He is all that satisfies! Sin has become a stranger as His presence overwhelms us. We are truly abiding in Him, as we willingly and joyfully follow Him. Our pursuit of Him has become much like a Song of Solomon pursuit of love, as we hide ourselves in the cleft of the rock or the secret place of the stairs:

Are You Abiding in the Word?

O my dove, that art in the clefts of the rock, in the secret places of the stairs, let me see thy countenance, let me hear thy voice; for sweet is thy voice, and thy countenance is comely.

Song of Solomon 2:14

Our Bridegroom is saying to us that He wants to hear our voice. He wants to commune with us and hear our praise and delight at His presence. The fruit of His love for us is sweet to the taste. He is the true Bread of Heaven:

O taste and see that the LORD is good: blessed is the man that trusteth in him.   Psalm 34:8

And the house of Israel called the name thereof Manna: and it was like coriander seed, white; and the taste of it was like wafers made with honey.   Exodus 16:31

Then Jesus said unto them, Verily, verily, I say unto you, Moses gave you not that bread from heaven; but my Father giveth you the true bread from heaven.   John 6:32

89

Bearing Fruit Without Ceasing

*How sweet are thy words unto my taste! yea,
sweeter than honey to my mouth!*
                                    Psalm 119:103

God wants us to return the love He has given us
again and again by way of His deeds and through
His Word. We praise Him as we realize that His love
is better than wine:

> *Let him kiss me with the kisses of his mouth: for
> thy love is better than wine.*
>   Song of Solomon 1:2

We worship when it is revealed to us that He has
brought us to His banqueting table:

> *He brought me to the banqueting house, and
> his banner over me was love.*
>   Song of Solomon 2:4

> *Thou preparest a table before me in the presence
> of mine enemies: thou anointest my head with
> oil; my cup runneth over.*   Psalm 23:5

He is our Beloved, and we are His. He is our Beloved, and His desire is toward us:

Are You Abiding in the Word?

My beloved is mine, and I am his: he feedeth among the lilies.   Song of Solomon 2:16

I am my beloved's, and his desire is toward me.
                                        Song of Solomon 7:10

He is the Bridegroom, and we have become His undefiled Bride:

> *I sleep, but my heart waketh: it is the voice of my beloved that knocketh, saying, Open to me, my sister, my love, my dove, my undefiled: for my head is filled with dew, and my locks with the drops of the night.* Song of Solomon 5:2

Our reliance upon Him and our need for Him seems to increase exponentially as time with Him in prayer, praise and study of His Word continues. Even our love for the Body of Christ increases and we gladly join with our brothers and sisters in Christ in fellowship and joint praise to God.

If all is right between you and God, all will be right between you and your brothers and sisters in Christ. Let's keep humble before Him and humble before the members of His Body. Never lose your first love! Keep this love alive and hold fast to Him. This is what it means to abide in Him!

Chapter 7

What Spirit Are You Led By?

A man's moral self shall be filled with the fruit of his mouth, and with the consequence of his words he must be satisfied [whether good or evil]. Proverbs 18:20-21, AMPC

It has been my observation that it is human nature to be solution oriented. Personally, I would learn one thing and practice that for a while, until I felt like I had grown beyond that and then move on to something else, usually some "higher learning" or, at least, I thought so at the time. Even if I didn't outwardly state it or actively think it, that was commonly the self-justification I gave myself. I have learned, however, that basic doctrinal understanding and simple truth is something we never grow out of, but, rather, something we build upon. One such doctrine is the use of confession as part of our established understanding of meditation. Thinking we could grow out of a basic truth is about as logical as believing that faith ended when the last original apostle died. That would be silly. Without a measure of faith, no one could be saved. Everyone knows that you must have faith just to get saved. So, if faith ended at that time, nobody since then would have been saved. That's how ridiculous it is to think you can grow beyond a basic truth.

I would also like to make a side note here: If I am being led by the Spirit of God, that leading will always be in agreement with and place the Word of God as Guide. The only thing that God is incapable of doing is lie. He will not, could not and never would contradict His own written holy Word.

It would be very easy to get far out of line from where God wants us, if we disregarded His Word, the Bible. I have seen many well-meaning Christians get off the right path because they either didn't know the Scriptures, misunderstood them or were wrestling against them—to their own destruction:

> *As also in all his epistles, speaking in them of these things; in which are some things hard to*

be understood, which they that are unlearned and unstable wrest, as they do also the other scriptures, unto their own destruction.

2 Peter 3:16

One of the most common wrong roads that people often have the misfortune to travel down is one that can easily mask a rebellious attitude or independent spirit. Let me clarify. I have often heard people quote some of the following scripture:

But the anointing which ye have received of him abideth in you: and ye need not that any man teach you: but as the same anointing teacheth you of all things, and is truth, and is no lie, and even as it hath taught you, ye shall abide in him. 1 John 2:27

I rarely hear people quote the whole scripture, but I have often heard the part that says nobody needs to teach them. It is usually quoted with an attitude that nobody can teach them because they already know it all. Even Christians who have had a measure of success in the progression of building what they believed to be the Kingdom of God need to position themselves with an attitude of humility toward their fellow believers. They might actually learn something. It is arrogance that says "I have no need that anyone teach me." It is arrogance when a person says that they hear from the Holy Spirit better than others. A house that is built on the pure Word of God is a humble house:

> *Finally, all [of you] should be of one and the same mind (united in spirit), sympathizing [with one another], loving [each other] as brethren [of one household], compassionate and courteous (tenderhearted and humble).*
>
> 1 Peter 3:8, AMPC

The scripture I previously mentioned, 1 John 2:27, in context and in keeping with the rest of the scriptures, does not mean that a man or woman filled with the Holy Spirit will not or cannot teach you. To believe that would be absolutely ridiculous. It would mean that every time a preacher delivered a message, you could not learn anything from it.

In addition to that, why would the Lord tell us, in Ephesians chapter 4, that He gave us apostles, prophets, evangelists, pastors and teachers to perfect the Body of Christ and for our edification, if we had no need of being taught by the Holy Spirit through them?

> *And he gave some, apostles; and some proph-*
> *ets; and some, evangelists; and some, pastors*
> *and teachers; tor the perfecting of the saints,*
> *for the work of the ministry, for the edifying of*
> *the body of Christ: till we all come in the unity*
> *of the faith, and of the knowledge of the Son of*
> *God, unto a perfect man, unto the measure of*
> *the stature of the fullness of Christ.*
>
> Ephesians 4:11-13

Please tell me, if you can, how these apostles, prophets, evangelists, pastors and teachers God has supplied are to do their job if you are not there to hear what they have to say? Perhaps you have been a Christian for some time now and have had a measure of success in building "His Kingdom." However, if you were motivated by an independent spirit and not by love for God as well as man and refused to allow yourself to be taught by any man, you have deceived yourself.

If you think you are being led by the Holy Spirit, and you are doing that, perhaps the question I should ask you might be, "What kind of spirit is leading you?" Maybe you are too busy doing the job of a scorner or critic or maybe you have become too busy "doing the works of God" to have a real relationship of intimacy with Him. Maybe it's time to repent and submit yourself to the plan the Lord of Hosts has for you.

Please understand me here. I am preaching to myself as well as to you. Let's look at what God tells us in Psalm 1:

> *Blessed is the man that walketh not in the counsel of the ungodly, nor standeth in the way of sinners, nor sitteth in the seat of the scornful. But his delight is in the law of the Lord; and in his law doth he meditate day and night.*
>
> Psalm 1:1-2

If a pastor forgets or is too busy to shake your hand, someone sat in "your" seat in church or your feelings were hurt in some way by a message that is preached or maybe you even embarrassed yourself in some way, that does *not* mean that it's time for you to go to some other church that you perceive might better meet your needs. It just means that it's time to nail your flesh to the cross and start getting serious with the Lord. Pride and vanity must die. Remember, the Lord of Hosts exalts the humble, not those who say or think how very important or great they are in comparison with others.

I once had the good fortune of hearing part of a message that a pastor in Taft, California preached concerning the Parable of the Fig Tree. His message was found in Luke 13:

> *He spake also this parable; A certain man had a fig tree planted in his vineyard; and he came and sought fruit thereon, and found none. Then said he unto the dresser of his vineyard, Behold, these three years I come seeking fruit on this fig tree, and find none: cut it down; why cumbereth it the ground? And he answering said unto him, Lord, let it alone this year also, till I shall dig about it, and dung it: And if it bear fruit, well: and if not, then after that thou shalt cut it down.* Luke 13:6-9

The point the pastor was making that interested me most was likening the vine dresser to an under-shepherd interceding for one of his flock. This is part of the job of an under-shepherd or pastor.

What Spirit Are You Led By?

Let me ask you a question: What are the chances that you will be interceded for if you are not in a local church and submitted to a pastor? The wise King Solomon declared: *"There is no new thing under the sun"* (Ecclesiastes 1:9). Your case is not original or even special. None of us is more important than another. Therefore, rules of submission apply to all of us. Submission to the authorities or under-shepherds God has placed over us to guard our souls makes their jobs so much easier. Why don't we just relax and trust the Lord?

The major part of unity in the Body of Christ is based on mutual submission that recognizes the presence of Christ in each member. We, then, can be kept, or bonded together, in peace and love, making us effectual workers for the Lord, truly submitted to and in Christ. We will never be able to grow *"unto the measure of the stature of the fullness of Christ"* until we submit ourselves in this way:

> *Till we all come to the unity of the faith and of the knowledge of the Son of God, to a perfect man, to the measure of the stature of the fullness of Christ.* Ephesians 4:13

Bearing Fruit Without Ceasing

I must tell you that truly mature Christians will be bearing much fruit. Let us keep ourselves on the mark and on God's highway.

Submission to the authorities or under-shepherds the Lord has placed over us is a necessary part of our growth as Christians. These leaders have been placed there to guard our souls. Why not make their jobs easier?

The major instruction in the making of this pie called the Body of Christ is the blending of the mixture, and this unity is based upon mutual submission that considers the ingredient of Christ in every part to be better than themselves. As we submit ourselves to one another, we are blended into an unstoppable mixture of His power.

Avoiding the ambition to lead will secure those who are called to lead in their positions of leadership. Leading with humility before God and each other will be leading with power. We must make a deliberate effort to stay vitally connected with the King in order to remain bonded in peace and love and in order that we may become or continue to be effectual workers for the Lord, truly rooted in Christ.

It is easy to sit here and offer up solutions, but the bottom line comes at the feet of our Savior. It is in the day of His power that all will be willing to follow and move in submission:

> *Thy people shall be willing in the day of thy power, in the beauties of holiness from the womb of the morning: thou hast the dew of thy youth.*
> Psalm 110:3

And that will happen as we abide in Him and lift up His name in praise. Praise the living Word of God, Jesus! Let's not be satisfied with praise that is not fervent, sweaty, joyous and delirious.

And remember, Jesus taught that the greatest among us will be the servant to all:

> *And whosoever of you will be the chiefest, shall be servant of all.*   Mark 10:44

Let's keep ourselves on the mark and be led by the Holy Spirit:

> *Say to them, that are of a fearful heart, Be strong, fear not: behold, your God will come with vengeance, even God with a recompense; he will come and save you. Then the eyes of*

the blind shall be opened, and the ears of the deaf shall be unstopped. Then shall the lame man leap as an hart, and the tongue of the dumb sing: for in the wilderness shall waters break out, and streams in the desert. And the parched ground shall become a pool, and the thirsty land springs of water: in the habitation of dragons, where each lay, shall be grass with reeds and rushes. And an highway shall be there, and a way, and it shall be called The way of holiness; the unclean shall not pass over it; but it shall be for those: the wayfaring men, though fools, shall not err therein. No lion shall be there, nor any ravenous beast shall go up thereon, it shall not be found there; but the redeemed shall walk there. Isaiah 35:4-9

Let's be led by the Holy Spirit and not by our emotions, our intellect or our flesh. Remember, the Bible doesn't say that as many as are led by *how they feel* are the sons of God. It doesn't say that as many as are led by *intelligence* are the sons of God, and it also doesn't say as many as are led by their *ambitions* are the sons of God. Instead, it says:

For as many as are led by the Spirit of God, they

What Spirit Are You Led By?

are the sons of God.   Romans 8:14

Don't forget, the Spirit and the Word agree. The Sword of the Spirit IS the Word of God:

> *And take the helmet of salvation, and the sword of the Spirit, which is the word of God.*
>   Ephesians 6:17

IF you are led by the Spirit of God, then YOU are a son of God! Rejoice in that knowledge.

Chapter 8

Are You Walking in True Holiness?

> *Keep thy heart with all diligence; for out of it are the issues of life. Put away from thee a froward mouth, and perverse lips put far from thee. Let thine eyes look right on, and let thine eyelids look straight before thee. Ponder the path of thy feet, and let all thy ways be established. Turn not to the right hand nor to the left: remove thy foot from evil.*   Proverbs 4:23-27

It is impossible to say enough about our need to walk in holiness:

> *Your testimonies are very sure; holiness [apparent in separation from sin, with simple trust*

Are You Walking in True Holiness?

and hearty obedience] is becoming to Your house, O LORD, forever.   Psalm 93:5, AMPC

For it is written, You shall be holy, for I am holy.   1 Peter 1:16

The original instance where that statement *"You shall be holy, for I am holy"* is in Leviticus 11:44-45. This holiness must NEVER be ignored. To ignore or disregard the holiness the Lord of Hosts requires is to ignore or disregard God Himself:

> *For God has not called us to impurity but to consecration [to dedicate ourselves to the most thorough purity]. Therefore whoever disregards (sets aside and rejects this) disregards not man but God, Whose [very] Spirit [Whom] He gives to you is holy (chaste, pure).*
> 1 Thessalonians 4:7-8, AMPC

Consider the love our heavenly Father has shown us by sending His Son. Should we trample the grace of the Lord under our feet in defiant deliberate sin or rebelliousness? Considering your daily life, attitudes and actions, what are the differences between you and an unbeliever? Is there any difference? Be honest with yourself. I'm not talking here about being bound up in religion; I'm talking about walking like Jesus. I'm not talking about comparing yourself with the worst person you know; I'm talking about seeing a difference in yourself, even from morally upright unbelievers.

And what is the measuring line? Christ is the measuring line. Where is the fruit of holiness in your life? That fruit will be equal to the dedication and submission you have toward Christ.

I can already hear the scorners crying, "Legalism! That's legalism!" But let me ask you something. Why is it that when holiness is talked about, that's always the first thing people say. If they drink alcohol and you indicate to them that drinking alcohol should be avoided, they cry, "Legalism! That's a religious spirit!" Some will even quote this passage from First Timothy:

> *Drink no longer water, but use a little wine for thy stomach's sake and thine often infirmities.*
>
> 1 Timothy 5:23

Most don't realize that this verse is, more than likely, referring to grape juice, not wine as we understand it today. Concerning wine, this is what the Bible says:

Are You Walking in True Holiness?

Wine is a mocker, strong drink is raging: and whosoever is deceived thereby is not wise.

Proverbs 20:1

Who hath woe? who hath sorrow? who hath contentions? who hath babbling? who hath wounds without cause? who hath redness of eyes? They that tarry long at the wine; they that go to seek mixed wine.   Proverbs 23:29-30

Nothing good can come of consuming wine.

If people smoke and you tell them that they should stop smoking, they cry, "Religious spirit!" If you tell them they need to be in church on Sundays, they may also object. If you tell them that they must repent of their homosexual behavior, they call you a hate monger or act like it is racism or intolerance (which is absolutely ridiculous). I refuse to be listed among those who ignore what the Bible clearly calls *"sin."*

The world has a sin problem, plain and simple, and I personally believe that the underlying reason legalism is brought up in so many cases is that the individuals speaking are masking their rebellion, while refusing to conform to the will of the Lord in their own hearts. When does the compromising stop? If you tell someone it's wrong to steal, they will probably agree with you. If you try to get people not to murder, they won't fight you. But try to get them to see the need to walk morally upright in every area of their lives, and then, suddenly, rebellion raises its ugly head, and they cry, "Legalism! Religious spirit! Intolerance! Hate-mongering!" They may even do this after they have fully agreed with *"Thou shalt not steal"* and *"Thou shalt not commit murder."* Can you see the contradiction there? May the Lord bless us with eyes that see.

Another important aspect of holiness is that it must begin on the inside of us. Do you seem holy on the outside, and yet inwardly you are consumed with bitterness and resentment? If so, it is time to forgive. An outward act of holiness or a good deed done for public viewing isn't the kind of holiness God wants from us. In fact, a pretended holiness stinks in His nostrils.

Many allow themselves to be influenced by a dead, Pharisee-type religion, but the Bible tells us that the Lord desires truth in the inmost parts of our being. In other words, He wants us to be honest with ourselves and with others:

> *Behold, thou desirest truth in the inward parts: and in the hidden part thou shalt make me to know wisdom.* Psalm 51:6

Are You Walking in True Holiness?

When people think of sin, they often think of immorality of various kinds. But one of the worst sins of which a large majority of people are guilty is the sin of unbelief. We may declare the love of God to others, but do we ourselves believe that He loves *us*? Really? We must be honest with ourselves.

Have you ever heard the expression "fallen from grace" used in Christian circles? I have often heard this phrase used in regard to people who have fallen into the sins of adultery or fornication. I was shocked when I discovered what Paul said (or, rather, *didn't* say) when he wrote to the Corinthian believers of the first century. He did not say to them, "You have fallen from grace." When Paul addressed the Galatians, He said something that surprised me:

> *Stand fast therefore in the liberty wherewith Christ hath made us free, and be not entangled again with the yoke of bondage. Behold, I Paul say unto you, that if ye be circumcised, Christ shall profit you nothing. For I testify again to every man that is circumcised, that he is a debtor to do the whole law. Christ is become of no effect unto you, whosoever of you are justified by the law; ye are fallen from grace.*
>
> Galatians 5:1-4

It was not those who were guilty of fornication whom Paul said had fallen from grace; it was those trying to justify themselves by the Law!

I confess that I have been guilty of the sin of unbelief. For years I thought that God was just waiting for me to make a mistake so that He could send a lightning bolt from Heaven to punish me. Then, the deeper my relationship with God became, the more I recognized His love for me and began accepting it as fact.

Prior to this, I had been in unbelief because I didn't fully accept the fact that God was a rewarder of those who diligently seek Him. I didn't believe He loved me, even though I knew that I loved Him. Why is this important? God's love is the basis for our faith. He so loved us and still does:

> *He who has My commandments and keeps them, it is he who loves Me. And he who loves Me will be loved by My Father, and I will love him and manifest Myself to him.*
>
> John 14:21

Let's be honest with ourselves and put away any form of sin, as we realize God's great love for us. That realization builds confidence and faith within us. Let's cleanse ourselves from all sin by the grace of God and His Holy Spirit, with true repentance:

Beloved, we are [even here and] now God's children; it is not yet disclosed (made clear) what we shall be [hereafter], but we know that when He comes and is manifested, we shall [as God's children] resemble and be like Him, for we shall see Him just as He [really] is. And everyone who has this hope [resting] on Him cleanses (purifies) himself just as He is pure (chaste, undefiled, guiltless). Everyone who commits (practices) sin is guilty of lawlessness; for [that is what] sin is lawlessness (the breaking, violating of God's law by transgression or neglect—being unrestrained and unregulated by His commands and His will).

1 John 3:2-4, AMPC

Another verse here in 1 John 3 also serves to clarify our position in regard to holiness:

No one who abides in Him [who lives and remains in communion with and in obedience to Him—deliberately, knowingly, and habitually] commits (practices) sin. No one

111

who [habitually] sins has either seen or known
Him [recognized, perceived, or understood Him,
or has had an experiential acquaintance with
Him].   1 John 3:6, AMPC

The point is that if you say with your own mouth, "Yes, Lord, I will follow You," and then, with your actions, you say something entirely different, who are you kidding? Please, for your own sake, make your "yes" mean "yes":

But let your communication be, Yea, yea; Nay,
nay; for whatsoever is more than these cometh
of evil.   Matthew 5:37

We need to be committed to doing what we have said we will do. Sin sickens the righteous heart. If you have compromised in your commitment to the Lord, repent of it and follow Him as you said you would:

What do you think? There was a man who had
two sons. He came to the first and said, Son
go and work today in the vineyard. And he
answered, I will not; but afterward he changed
his mind and went. Then the man came to the

Are You Walking in True Holiness?

second and said the same [thing]. And he re-
plied, I will [go], sir; but he did not go. Which
of the two did the will of the father?
They replied, The first one.
Jesus said to them, Truly I tell you, the tax collec-
tors and harlots will get into the kingdom of heaven
before you. Matthew 21:28-31, AMPC

Let us answer the call to work in the vineyard of our lives and then the lives of others, producing all manner of fruit and pleasure for the Owner of the vineyard in Whom our soul delights. We can be consistent as we order our lives in His way by His Spirit. The best Friend and Companion we could ever have is the Holy Spirit. Ask Him to help you by giving you a reverential fear of God. This will produce the needed results:

> *The fear of the Lord is to hate evil: pride, and*
> *arrogancy, and the evil way, and the froward*
> *mouth, do I hate.* Proverbs 8:13

Remember to pray. Pray in the Spirit and in all other manner of prayers. Fasting and prayer could do us all some good. Get that flesh crucified! Fast and pray, and confess God's Word! Fast and pray, confess His Word, pray His Word, say His Word and shout His Word. Most of all, LOVE and obey His Word:

Hear, for I will speak excellent and princely things; and the opening of my lips shall be for right things. For my mouth shall utter truth, and wrongdoing is detestable and loathsome to my lips. All the words of my mouth are righteous (upright and in right standing with God); there is nothing contrary to truth or crooked in them. They are all plain to him who understands [and opens his heart], and right to those who find knowledge [and live by it]. Receive my instruction in preference to [striving for] silver, and knowledge rather than choice gold, For skillful and godly Wisdom is better than rubies or pearls, and all the things that may be desired are not to be compared to it.

Proverbs 8:6-11, AMPC

Chapter 9

Are You Manifesting God's Love?

Clothe yourselves therefore as (God's own picked representatives,) His own chosen ones, [who are purified and holy and well-beloved [by God Himself, by putting on behavior marked by] tenderhearted pity and mercy, kind feeling, a lowly opinion of yourselves, gentle ways, [and] patience—which is tireless, long-suffering and has the power to endure whatever comes, with good temper. Be gentle and forbearing with one another and, if one has a difference (a grievance or complaint) against another, readily pardoning each other; even as the Lord has forgiven you, so must you also [forgive.] And above all these [put on] love and enfold yourselves with the bond of perfectness—which binds everything together completely in ideal harmony.

Colossians 3:12-14, AMPC

For some, this might seem like an odd place to talk about love. You might ask, "Why would you address the issue of love when addressing the subject of holiness?" Let me endeavor to explain.

Paul wrote this third chapter of Colossians in his letter to the early believers there. And, in this verse 14, we find the phrase *"the bond of perfectness."* What does it mean? To see this truth more clearly, let's examine what the King James Version of the Bible says in the same verse:

> *And above all these things put on charity, which*
> *is the bond of perfectness.*   Colossians 3:14

What is *charity*? In most modern versions of the Bible, this word is translated as *love*. The New International Version, for example, uses the phrase: *"over all these virtues put on love."* This verse demonstrates the reason I want to talk about love in connection with holiness. Love is *"the bond of perfectness."*

We know that the fulfilling of the Law would have been an example of absolute holiness and perfection. However, no one could accomplish it. The good news is that the Lord Jesus Christ illustrated that perfect man of holiness by fulfilling and living the

Are You Manifesting God's Love?

Law perfectly. He did this for our sakes, for we were incapable of doing it on our own:

> *For as by one mans disobedience many were made sinners, so by the obedience of one shall many be made righteous.* Romans 5:19

Jesus gave righteousness to us who believe:

> *For if by one man's offence death reigned by one; much more they which receive abundance of grace and of the gift of righteousness shall reign in life by one, Jesus Christ.* Romans 5:17

Jesus commanded us to love one another:

> *A new commandment I give unto you, That ye love one another; as I have loved you, that ye also love one another.* John 13:34

Jesus then showed that if we love Him we must obey Him:

> *If you love me keep my commandments.*
> John 14:15

It is by faith in the Lord Jesus Christ that we *"establish the law"*:

> *Do we then make void the law through faith?*
> *God forbid: yea, we establish the law.*
>
> Romans 3:31

It is by obedience to Christ's commandments that we *"fulfill the law"*:

> *Owe no man any thing, but to love one another:*
> *for he that loveth another hath fulfilled the law.*
>
> Romans 13:8

The Law illustrated holiness and perfection in its fulfillment (brought by the Lord Jesus Christ) and Romans 13:8 shows that we, too, can come to illustrate holiness and perfection by *"lov[ing] one another"* as we ought.

The Bible tells us that God is love, and that if we don't love, we don't even know Him:

> *He who does not love has not become acquainted*
> *with God—does not and never did know Him;*
> *for God is love.*   1 John 4:8, AMPC

Are You Manifesting God's Love?

The very first fruit of the Spirit listed in Galatians 5 is love:

> *But the fruit of the Spirit is love, joy, peace, long-suffering, gentleness, goodness, faith, meekness, temperance: against such there is no law.* Galatians 5:22-23

Our primary pursuit has been set before us, and that goal is to acquire or possess love:

> *Eagerly pursue and seek to acquire [this] love—make it your aim, your great quest.*
> 1 Corinthians 14:1, AMPC

The King James Version says *"follow after charity,"* the New American Standard Version says *"PURSUE LOVE,"* and the New International Version says, *"Follow the way of love."* Since we are to pursue love, it makes sense that we should acquaint ourselves with the biblical definition of love.

The Lord of Hosts *is* love, and He was personally present in Christ, reconciling the world to Himself:

> *To wit, that God was in Christ, reconciling the world unto himself, not imputing their trespasses*

*unto them; and hath committed unto us the word
of reconciliation.* 2 Corinthians 5:19

Therefore, we know that the Lord Jesus Christ
is love and that love was incarnated in the flesh.
Still, He was the same person Who denounced the
Pharisees:

*Ye serpents, ye generation of vipers, how can
ye escape the damnation of hell?*
Matthew 23:33

Jesus had previously said to them:

*Woe unto you, scribes and Pharisees, hypo-
crites! for ye are like unto whited sepulchers,
which indeed appear beautiful outward, but
are within full of dead men's bones, and of all
uncleanness. Even so ye also outwardly appear
righteous unto men, but within ye are full of
hypocrisy and iniquity.* Matthew 23:27-28

Love rejoices in and because of truth, and is not
afraid to tell it like it is.

Let's take a closer look at the Bible definition of
love (which is its best definition).

Are You Manifesting God's Love?

Love endures long and is patient and kind; love never is envious nor boils over with jealousy; is not boastful or vainglorious, does not display itself haughtily. It is not conceited—arrogant and inflated with pride; it is not rude (unmannerly), and does not act unbecomingly. Love [God's love in us] does not insist on its' own rights or its' own way, for it is not self-seeking; it is not touchy or fretful or resentful; it takes no account of the evil done to it—pays no attention to a suffered wrong. It does not rejoice at injustice and unrighteousness, but rejoices when right and truth prevail. Love bears up under anything and everything that comes, is ever ready to believe the best of every person, its hopes are fadeless under all circumstances and it endures everything [without weakening]. Love never fails—never fades out or becomes obsolete or comes to an end.

1 Corinthians 13:4-8a, AMPC

A thorough investigation of 1 Corinthians 13:4-8 quickly determines that the character of love is actually the epitome or height of holiness. Therefore, over the next few pages, I will attempt to examine, at least to some degree, this passage.

"Love endures long and is patient" informs us of the endurance and patience of love. This is just one of the attributes that the love from the Lord produces in us. The Lord waited patiently for you and me to come to repentance and receive His Son as our Savior. You and I need to have and exercise patience so that we are able, by His Spirit, to take charge of our own soul (emotions and intellect):

In your patience possess ye your souls.

Luke 21:19

In order to show us more clearly what it means to be patient or enduring, most of us could look to our mothers as an example. My mother wasn't happy at all the day I, as a seventeen-year-old boy, signed up to join the U.S. Navy. With this act, I began a life of sin that was a great disappointment to her, and I know I was also a disappointment to the Lord. My mother waited patiently and endured this period that so many call "sowing your wild oats" and was glad when I finally said to her one day, "I'm through with that 'stuff'! I am born gain now!" Praise the Lord for patient mothers!

How often we lose patience with our brethren. Someone is struggling along, and they are not quick enough for us. We've seen how long they've had that problem, and we say, "Enough is enough!" Our Lord expects that we develop His patience in us. Love is patient. Patience is a quality of Christ, Who was and is holy.

"Love ... is ... kind." To me, kindness is the opposite of cruelty. How many people have you met who had a so-called "holiness" but lacked compassion? That was the reason Jesus told the Pharisees to go learn about mercy. Kindness is merciful:

> *But go ye and learn what that meaneth, I will have mercy, and not sacrifice: for I am not come to call the righteous, but sinners to repentance.*
> Matthew 9:13

Sinners know that they are sinners when they come into the presence of the Holy Spirit. Jesus overcame the sin of those He met with His kindness, and He is holiness exemplified. If we are not in true holiness, we might find ourselves condemning those who are not even guilty:

> *For if ye had known what this meaneth, I will have mercy, and not sacrifice, ye would not have condemned the guiltless.* Matthew 12:7

Love *"never is envious nor boils over with jealousy."* Envy or jealousy is a work of the flesh and has been the weapon used most often against the leaders in the Body of Christ. The enemy of our souls utilizes this fleshly quality in order to facilitate his purposes. If you find yourself even a little jealous or envious of others, you're not abiding in genuine love.

The dictionary defines *jealous* as "afraid, suspicious, resentful, of rivalry in the affection or on the part of a spouse." This says that real love, which is the love of and from God, is not afraid of rivalry, suspicious of rivalry or resentful of rivalry. In fact, if a brother or sister in Christ has become a rival to you, then you need to let them win. Become a cheerleader for the success and accomplishments of others, not a critic.

It was pride that was first found in Satan and then jealousy. Satan was jealous of the worship God received. Personally, I don't remember ever being jealous, but I have had enough other fleshly problems to more than make up for it. I've had church folks force their way or will in church and in the process berate me to justify themselves. The way you handle folks like that is by not handling them, but, instead, letting the Lord of Hosts handle them. Our job is just to love and forgive.

Are You Manifesting God's Love?

Let us each do our part in keeping the unity of the faith. Love is not envious or jealous. Instead, love congratulates success. The lack of envy or jealousy is a vital part of possessing a holy character.

Love is *"not boastful or vainglorious, does not display itself haughtily. It is not conceited—arrogant and inflated with pride."* Here is where the enemy of our souls fell. It is so very important that we know most assuredly that pride or vanity in any form stinks in the nostrils of the Lord. Of the many problems that Christians face, the problem of vanity is just as bad (and is probably rated right alongside of) fornication in the church. In fact, if sin had a rating of what is bad to what is worst, I think pride would be pretty close to the top. Or should I say the bottom?

This problem is quite common in the Body of Christ today. I believe it is very important to know who the Lord says you are, but it is equally important to know that it is all the Lord's doing, not yours. Is it any wonder that the power of the Lord is not as evident as it should be in our lives?

Many prophecies based upon vanity and pride go forth these days, and they are only an imitation of the real thing. There are also many self-proclaimed prophets and self-proclaimed apostles, and these seem to say to a lost world that it is foolish to believe in the God of Abraham, Isaac and Jacob, for He clearly has no power. Self-proclamations without the fruit to back them up are vain. Worse, they are stains and blotches on the Church they pretend to represent. If you are one of the pretenders, it's not too late to repent and be restored.

Always remember that vanity, in even the smallest measure, is sin. Love doesn't seek a title. Love doesn't need to be the boss. Love is not proud. The absence of boasting, conceit or pride is another characteristic of true holiness.

Love is *"not rude (unmannerly) and does not act unbecomingly"* and love *"does not insist on its own rights or its own way."* The fact that love is *"not rude"* tells me that it is polite or courteous.

This reminds of an experience I had many years ago in Hong Kong. It was my first time to visit that amazing city, I was trying to get acclimated to their public transportation system, and it was quite a shock. I was standing in a line of folks waiting for the KCR (Kowloon-Canton Railway, an above-ground electric-driven train). When the KCR finally came into the station and stopped, people began to push their way toward the opening doors. I politely allowed those who seemed to be in such a great hurry to go ahead of me. But, to my surprise, I was nearly left behind. Everyone seemed perfectly content to push their way past me and leave me standing there. Love is *"not rude."* Love does not say "me first." Not acting *"unbecomingly"* could include all manner of behavior that would illustrate an obvious holiness.

The dictionary defines *unbecoming* as "not suited to the wearer." Such behavior could be anything that does not illustrate the proper behavior for a saint. We cannot be in compromise and see this point clearly. If *unbecoming* is "not suited to the wearer," then *becoming* means "something that *is* suited to the wearer." An outfit that is *becoming* would fit the wearer in size, color and status.

Our status is that we are *"seated in heavenly places"* in Christ and, therefore, acting rude or unbecomingly is not fitting to that position. Insisting on our own way or running to be first in a buffet line is rooted in the rebellious nature of the flesh.

The first thing we often notice in a child is the I-want attitude, and growing up isn't always easy. I've known some to keep that I-want attitude years after being born again. The sad result is that they are led by their emotions and intellect and not by the Spirit of God. Usually, in fact, the I-want attitude leads us in the opposite direction of the Spirit of God.

Some of these people are well meaning, but we cannot insist on our own way and, at the same time, follow the ways of Christ. We must learn to yield to the Master, giving Him first place in our lives.

Isn't it wonderful that Jesus is still working on perfecting His Saints (you and me)?

> *But Jesus called them unto him, and said, Ye know that the princes of the Gentiles exercise dominion over them, and they that are great exercise authority upon them. But it shall not be so among you: but whosoever will be great among you, let him be your minister; and whosoever will be chief among you, let him be your servant: even as the Son of man came not to be ministered unto, but to minister, and to give his life a ransom for many.*   Matthew 20:25-28

If we are more concerned about the needs of others, it will be less likely that we will be concerned about ourselves or our "rights." Love *"does not insist on its own rights."* Once a holy character is molded into our lives, we will no longer be rude or insist on having things our own way.

Love *"is not touchy or fretful or resentful; it takes no account of the evil done to it—pays no attention to a suf-*

fered wrong." Early in my Christian walk, I learned something about being touchy. I had been growing stronger and stronger in the anointing, but then a problem of ego came to the surface. Did you ever notice that the disciples had no problem with thoughts of their own greatness until after they had begun to be used by the Lord?

> *Then James and John, the sons of Zebedee, came to Him, saying, "Teacher, we want You to do for us whatever we ask."*
> *And He said to them, "What do you want Me to do for you?"*
> *They said to Him, "Grant us that we may sit, one on Your right hand and the other on Your left, in Your glory.*   Mark 10:35-37, NKJV

One day, while I was worshipping our Lord Jesus Christ, with my hands uplifted, I seemed to be ascending higher and higher. Then someone next to me put their hands up, and one of their hands bounced onto my nose. When this happened, I immediately lost all my so-called holiness. I thought, "This guy is so rude!" In time I realized that I was being "touchy."

Love *"is not ... fretful."* This term *fretful* means "worried." Before I was born again, I used to think I was going to die if I experienced any unusual physical symptom. But worry is silly, isn't it?

Love *"is not resentful."* Being resentful used to be a common part of my life. Before I was born again, if a person even looked at me wrong, I was sometimes resentful. Resentment has often tried to have its way with me. If I really wanted to, I could find many things to be resentful about, but because of the new nature that dwells in me, I no longer want to do that.

Oh, I have suffered injustice, even within the Body of Christ. Some people have shown contempt toward me, but since resentment is not a luxury a born-again Christian can possess, I don't let it bother me. Think of the worst thing another human being could do to you, and I have probably suffered it or, at least, felt that I did. But now nothing is worthy of resentment. We should simply ignore the things that try to distract us, even when someone treats us wrongfully. If what they have said is bad enough, it will catch up with them. We need to overlook sins against us.

As a young Christian, I once went to a church with the idea of helping that church. (This was only my idea and was not inspired or led by the Lord.) As I listened to the preacher that day, he said something to which I took offense. He must have known this, for after the service he looked at me as we were shaking hands and said, "The Spirit of God is not easily offended."

My first thought was, "Is that scriptural?"

Immediately the Spirit of God within me replied, "Doesn't the Bible say that God is love?"

I answered, "Yes."

Then the Spirit of God within me said, "Since you know this is true, tell me what does the Bible say in 1 Corinthians 13? Doesn't it say that love is not easily provoked?"

I again answered, but this time with much more reverence, "Yes, Lord."

Again the Spirit of God said, "Now, God is a Spirit isn't He?"

Again, I said, "Yes, Lord."

The Spirit of God continued, "Therefore, the Spirit of God is not easily offended."

I answered, "Yes, Lord, and please forgive me for being offensive to You."

The Scripture in 1 Corinthians 13 that the Spirit of God in me quoted was from verse 5 in the King James Version of the Bible: *"Love ... is not easily provoked."*

Then, with my more enlightened understanding of 1 Corinthians 13:5, I was able to measure all my future behavior alongside of it. If I began to get angry, I would immediately put the measuring line of scripture next to it. In the process, I also learned that getting angry did not help me to be righteous:

> For the wrath of man worketh not the righteousness of God.   James 1:20

Now, I could no longer be what some termed "righteously indignant" and do it in good conscience. Love is not "holier than thou;" it's humble. Love is not *"resentful"* and *"takes no account of a suffered wrong"* and this is also another mark of a truly holy life.

Love *"does not rejoice at injustice and unrighteousness, but rejoices when right and truth prevail."* Looking at this part of 1 Corinthians 13 reminds me of what the Bible says about wisdom. It is wisdom speaking in the following scripture:

> *I, Wisdom [from God], make prudence my dwelling, and I find out knowledge and discretion. The reverent fear and worshipful awe of the LORD [includes] the hatred of evil; pride, arrogance, the evil way, and perverted and twisted speech I hate. I have counsel and sound knowledge, I have understanding, I have might*

*and power. By me kings reign and rulers decree
justice.*   Proverbs 8:12-15, AMPC

If you read down a few more verses, you will find
that righteousness is with wisdom:

*Riches and honor are with me, enduring wealth
and righteousness (uprightness in every area
and relation, and right standing with God).*
                    Proverbs 8:18, AMPC

Earlier I was quoting Jesus as He rebuked the
Pharisees. It was also established that the Lord Jesus
Christ is love. Love always gets happy when the
truth has first place in our lives. I love the written
Word of God, but, most of all, I love the One Who is
the Word of God. If we don't love the truth, we will
not be admitted to Heaven:

*And with all deceivableness of unrighteousness
in them that perish; because they received not
the love of the truth, that they might be saved.*
                    2 Thessalonians 2:10

Love *"does not rejoice at injustice and unrighteousness, but rejoices when right and truth prevail,"* and

this is an obvious quality of holiness. To abide in true love is to abide in the love that comes from the Lord, and by abiding in the love that comes from the Lord, we will also be abiding in Him Who *is* the Truth, Jesus Himself.

Love *"bears up under anything and everything that comes."* We must learn this aspect of love so that we do not grow weary in well doing:

> *And let us not be weary in well doing: for in due season we shall reap, if we faint not.*
>
> Galatians 6:9

With an attitude of love, we can rise up even after having fallen on our face in the dirt. You will be able to spit out the dirt and get up with a smile:

> *For a just man falleth seven times, and riseth up again: but the wicked fall into mischief.*
>
> Proverbs 24:16

Have you ever loved someone and seen what God had planned for them? Well, the knowing of His plan for them can often help you to look past the lousy ways they may be treating you. Seeing things or people in the way God sees them can make it so much easier for His love to flow through us to them. We are able to bear up under whatever circumstances may be presented.

Look at the life of Paul. He went through plenty of hardship for the sake of love:

> *Of the Jews five times received I forty stripes save one. Thrice was I beaten with rods, once was I stoned, thrice I suffered shipwreck, a night and a day I have been in the deep; in journeyings often, in perils of waters, in perils of robbers, in perils by mine own countrymen, in perils by the heathen, in perils in the city, in perils in the wilderness, in perils in the sea, in perils among false brethren; in weariness and painfulness, in watchings often, in hunger and thirst, in fastings often, in cold and nakedness. Beside those things that are without, that which cometh upon me daily, the care of all the churches.*
>
> 2 Corinthians 11:24-28

We need to develop a tenacity in the Spirit of God that has staying power. Staying power can be found in the love God generates within us. This love can be fanned to a flame and embedded deep into the coals of the altar of the Lord of Hosts in us.

Bearing Fruit Without Ceasing

The prophet Hosea was told to marry a prostitute. In this way, he went through what the Lord has gone through with some of us, as we went prostituting ourselves after the many other gods of self-centered ambition, self-aggrandizement and intellectualized pursuit, as well as the pursuit of our own lusts—to name only a few. Praise the Lord! He forgives and restores, as we repent and turn from sin!

Let's learn to bear up under all circumstances. As for me and my house, we will *"bear up under anything and everything that comes"* for Jesus' sake through His love. Can you see the quality of holiness in *"bearing up"* under whatever comes our way?

Love is *"ever ready to believe the best of every person."* This is a tough one. The first thing that comes to mind is the tendency of the human race (myself included) to be judgmental. I have met thousands of Christians with so-called "discerning of spirits." What they really had was a bad case of the critic-isms. Something was wrong with everyone, and they could tell you what it was—if you asked them. Even if you didn't ask them, they would probably tell you whether you liked it or not. The skeptical nature of the flesh is the dominating factor in their lives and not the Holy Spirit.

The Holy Spirit is grieved when we falsely accuse and judge others. In both the book of Matthew and the book of Luke, Jesus is quoted as saying *"judge not."* Let's look at what was stated by Matthew:

> *Judge not, that ye be not judged. For with what judgment ye judge, ye shall be judged; and with what measure ye mete, it shall be measured to you again.*   Matthew 7:1-2

I believe that Jesus didn't *"judge;"* He only repeated what He heard the Holy Spirit saying:

> *Ye judge after the flesh; I judge no man. And yet if I judge, my judgment is true: for I am not alone, but I and the Father that sent me.*
> John 8:15-16

The heart of this issue of being *"ever ready to believe the best of every person"* is not addressed at its core if we are only *not* judging someone. If we have an attitude that excludes passing judgment on others, that's good, but it is not the desired goal. The intent of this passage of scripture in 1 Corinthians 13 reaches even higher. It means that in replacement of an attitude of criticism, we have a positive attitude and outlook toward other people.

You cannot ever, as the expression goes, judge a book by its cover. When we truly love with the love that comes from God, we will have no fear of man:

> *The fear of man bringeth a snare: but whoso putteth his trust in the LORD shall be safe.*
>
> Proverbs 29:25

> *There is no fear in love; but perfect love casteth out fear: because fear hath torment. He that feareth is not made perfect in love.*
>
> 1 John 4:18

Another example in scripture that could help us to walk in love can be found in Philippians:

> *Finally, brethren, whatsoever things are true, whatsoever things are honest, whatsoever things are just, whatsoever things are pure, whatsoever things are lovely, whatsoever things are of good report; if there be any virtue, and if there be any praise, think on these things.*
>
> Philippians 4:8

Our focus will be on what is important to us. Using Philippians 4:8 as a guide, we can look for what is true, honest, just, pure, lovely, of good report, virtuous or praiseworthy in the people we meet. If we look deep enough, we may see Jesus. Of course, it's not always that easy, but the point is that we make the choice to love. Do you *"believe the best of every person?"* If you do, you are exhibiting another attribute of holiness.

Love's *"hopes are fadeless under all circumstances and it endures everything [without weakening]. Love never fails—never fades out or becomes obsolete or comes to an end."* Without the hope of salvation, we would all be in a sad state. *Hope* defined means "expectation and desire (of thing), trust." Once, when I saw this simple trust displayed in an adult, I thought to myself, "How naive he is!" Yet, when seeing this same simple trust in a child, I thought, "That is so beautiful!" What was the difference between the two? Should I expect that the adult would not be trusting and the child would?

Shouldn't we expect people to try to take advantage of us? Shouldn't we protect ourselves? The simplicity of trusting someone typically illustrates the gentle nature of the Holy Spirit. Maybe you look at someone who is trusting as if they are stupid, knowing nothing. That actually shows your own arrogance. Just because someone demonstrates trust in their nature does not mean they are gullible. I was wrong to make such a judgment of the man I just described who had the simple trust.

Love is a very solid structure upon which we can build, because the Lord of Hosts *is* love. He never fails, and He will always exist. Remember, if we love one another as the Lord would have us to, we fulfill the Law, and the fulfillment of the Law brings with it a demonstration of holiness.

Following this explanation of love, you need to know one very important fact. It is impossible for us to love as the Lord of Hosts wants us to love unless His love is flowing through us. The good news is that we have His love in us, as a born-again child of the Lord. So, as we submit ourselves to His presence in us, it is natural for us to love and obey.

What is the Lord asking us to do? He wants us to trust Him and submit to His leading. Let us, therefore, submit to the true leading of His Holy Spirit:

> *And hope maketh not ashamed; because the love of God is shed abroad in our hearts by the Holy Ghost which is given unto us.* Romans 5:5

Loves *"hopes are fadeless"* and *"love never fails."* The Lord of Hosts *is* love, and LOVE (His love in us) is

Are You Manifesting God's Love?

Holy! He is Love, and that makes Love Holy! Holy! Holy!

> *In the year that king Uzziah died I saw also the LORD sitting upon a throne, high and lifted up, and his train filled the temple. Above it stood the seraphims: each one had six wings; with twain he covered his face, and with twain he covered his feet, and with twain he did fly. And one cried unto another, and said, Holy, holy, holy, is the LORD of hosts: the whole earth is full of his glory. And the posts of the door moved at the voice of him that cried, and the house was filled with smoke. Then said I, Woe is me! for I am undone; because I am a man of unclean lips, and I dwell in the midst of a people of unclean lips: for mine eyes have seen the King, the LORD of hosts. Then flew one of the seraphims unto me, having a live coal in his hand, which he had taken with the tongs from off the altar: And he laid it upon my mouth, and said, Lo, this hath touched thy lips; and thine iniquity is taken away, and thy sin purged.* Isaiah 6:1-7

Chapter 10

Are You Working Out Your Own Salvation?

Do not allow your mouth to cause your body to sin, and do not say before the messenger [the priest] that it was an error or mistake. Why should God be [made] angry at your voice and destroy the work of your hands?

Ecclesiastes 5:6, AMPC

When I was much younger, I first heard Philippians 2:12 from the King James Version of the Bible:

Wherefore, my beloved, as ye have always obeyed, not as in my presence only, but now much more in my absence, work out your own salvation with fear and trembling. Philippians 2:12

Are You Working Out Your Own Salvation?

After having heard this Scripture thundered from a few pulpits, I didn't think I could ever be saved, and this brought me great despair. I just knew that I would never be able to make it to Heaven. Even after I had been born again, this scripture continued to baffle me. I couldn't imagine how I was ever going to make it.

Then one day I heard this verse in its simplicity through a pastor I deeply admired and respected. He was Pastor George Stover, and he explained this verse far better than I ever could. I will attempt to summarize his meaning here.

The seed of hope or our salvation is the Lord Jesus Christ, the Word of God. In order for the world to see Jesus, this salvation must make its way from the inside of us to the outside of us. Thus, we "work out" or project outward our salvation. The fear and trembling mentioned here comes because of the reverence we learn as we yield our soul (emotions and intellect) to the work of the Holy Spirit.

If we give every part of our bodies to the Lord, holding nothing back, and if we give all of our mind to the Lord, trusting Him, then we will be following the plan the Lord has for each of us.

Paul wrote to the Roman believers:

I appeal to you therefore, brethren, and beg of you in view of [all] the mercies of God, to make a decisive dedication of your bodies [presenting all your members and faculties] as a living sacrifice, holy (devoted, consecrated) and well pleasing to God, which is your reasonable (rational, intelligent) service and spiritual worship. Do not be conformed to this world (this age), [fashioned after and adapted to its external, superficial customs], but be transformed (changed) by the [entire] renewal of your mind [by its new ideals and its new attitude], so that you may prove [for yourselves] what is the good and acceptable and perfect will of God, even the thing which is good and acceptable and perfect [in His sight for you].

Romans 12:1-2, AMPC

It is easier to understand what is meant by "working out your salvation" if you have a basic comprehension of your spirit, soul and body and how they relate to the Spirit of God. There are good books available on this subject, especially in the Faith Movement circles, that make the relationship between the Spirit of God and our spirit, soul and body quite clear. I will endeavor to explain this relationship in a very limited measure.

Are You Working Out Your Own Salvation?

When you and I heard the Gospel message, the Spirit of God was moving upon us, in order to convince us of the truth of the message. The Spirit was working on our soul, which is comprised of our emotions and intellect, in order to convince us. We had the choice of accepting or rejecting the message. Upon accepting the need for repentance that goes along with the Gospel message, we received the Lord Jesus Christ as Savior and Leader of our life. As we confessed with our mouth the Lord Jesus Christ, the Spirit of the Lord recreated each of our spirits individually. We became a new creation. We were born again:

> *Therefore if any person is [ingrafted] in Christ (the Messiah) he is a new creation (a new creature altogether); the old [previous moral and spiritual condition] has passed away. Behold, the fresh and new has come!*
>
> 2 Corinthians 5:17, AMPC

You are the one who became *"a new creation."* The real you, as an individual, is spirit. We each have a soul, comprised of our emotions and intellect, and, lastly, we live in a body made of flesh, bones and blood. The Bible mentions the spirit, soul and body in 1 Thessalonians:

Bearing Fruit Without Ceasing

And the very God of peace sanctify you wholly; and I pray God your whole spirit and soul and body be preserved blameless unto the coming of our Lord Jesus Christ. 1 Thessalonians 5:23

The goal for each one of us is, by conscious choice, to make our soul to walk in obedience to our spirit and to make our body to walk in obedience to our soul, by the crucifixion of the sinful nature of our flesh, with the help of the Holy Spirit. As we decide, with resolve, to discipline our souls with the washing of the water of the Word of God, while walking it out in obedience, the Holy Spirit helps us. The result is that our salvation is "worked out."

Without your body, you would still exist. If you were a born-again, obedient child of God and your body died, you would go up into Heaven. If you were not a born-again child of God, you would go down to Hell, and the Bible confirms this. The body, which is often referred to as a "vessel of clay or earth," cannot inherit the heavenly blessing of communion with God, because of the corrupt nature or sin nature inherited from Adam:

Are You Working Out Your Own Salvation?

Now this I say, brethren, that flesh and blood cannot inherit the kingdom of God; neither doth corruption inherit incorruption.

1 Corinthians 15:50

The soul is what we are to wash with the Word of God. Meditating upon His Word not only cleanses the soul, but it also feeds the spirit. As we fellowship with the Holy Ghost, repeatedly filling our soul with the Word of God, our mind is renewed, and our spirit man gets stronger and stronger. Revelation comes from the Holy Ghost, after persistent and continued exposure to the Word of God. This brings a progressively greater revelation of His Word, and, as a result, we have greater freedom:

Then said Jesus to those Jews which believed on him, If ye continue in my word, then are ye my disciples indeed; and ye shall know the truth and the truth shall make you free.

John 8:31-32

Continually repeating and studying the Word activates the spirit, the real you. The Holy Spirit activates the Word of God to our spirit, making it more alive. I once went over one verse of scripture for an entire day. Then, suddenly it became so alive to me that I was in amazement. Revelation poured into me, connecting that scripture with many others. That is what I'm talking about here. We need to be persistent!

Let me tell you: once the Word of God is grasped in the spirit and it is quickened to the soul, there isn't a force in Hell that can take that understanding away from you. Once the Word takes on revelation to us, it will always be with us.

Working outward our salvation needs to be done with great reverence. As we get to know the Lord Jesus Christ through the written holy Word of God, through prayer and fellowship with the Holy Spirit, and in our everyday life, as a born-again child of God, walking in obedience to the Law of love, we will realize and see more and more of His majesty, His holiness, His vastness, His loveliness, His kindness and His grace. With just a small amount of this understanding, we can see the great need for reverentially working outward God's presence in our lives.

Now, I want you to know what I didn't know as a young Christian. Here it is. Are you ready? The working outward of our salvation is a work of the Spirit of God. Our job is just to cooperate.

Are You Working Out Your Own Salvation?

Perhaps what I just wrote could be more easily understood in a different way. Our job is to submit to the Vine and bow before the Husbandman and His working in our lives:

> *I am the true vine, and my Father is the husbandman. Every branch in me that beareth not fruit he taketh away: and every branch that beareth fruit, he purgeth it, that it may bring forth more fruit.*   John 15:1-2

A branch doesn't do anything special; it just holds firmly to the vine. That branch doesn't strain to bear fruit. The branch simply holds fast to the vine, and the strength of the vine, and the vine, which provides life-giving sap, energizing that branch. In our case, the Vine is holy, and because of the life-giving sap and the fact that the branch is vitally connected to the Vine, the branch has inherited that holiness.

This works only when the branch of any tree is identified with that tree and has the inherent nature of the vine of its origin. For example, the branch of a peach tree is not called an orange tree, is it? In that same way, you and I must bear the name of Christ, the True Vine, the Vine of our origin. Any fruit we bear is because of Him:

Bearing Fruit Without Ceasing

For if the firstfruit be holy, the lump is also holy:
and if the root be holy, so are the branches.

Romans 11:16

In our case, the branch is totally dependent upon the Vine, and it doesn't rest upon another branch, lest the Husbandman come ready to prune it. If that branch is found to be resting on the arm of flesh for its strength, it will be pruned. The eyes of the Husbandman gaze upon the Vine much as the eyes of an artist who knows ahead of time what his painting will look like upon completion.

When pruning time comes, a cut here and another cut there seem to be so pointless to the branch, which has no understanding of the process and what is anticipated as a result. Although it is stinging from the cut, the branch remains in place, and the Husbandman applies some soothing oil of grace upon the wounds of misunderstanding.

"The Husbandman is trustworthy, and the Vine can be trusted. You can rest fully upon Him," this branch may say to you. Another branch might be heard commenting, "Listen to the Vine and receive His love." Perhaps a branch of great size and strength could be heard to say, "The fruit will come. Be patient to wait for it." Messages of encouragement might be heard throughout the whole community of branches if we could but listen to their prophetic utterance.

Even the True Vine can be heard speaking to us, as the life-giving sap that flows from Him begins to flow through us. As we listen to His Voice deep within us, we might hear the following:

> *If ye abide in me, and my words abide in you, ye shall ask what ye will, and it shall be done unto you. Herein is my Father glorified, that ye bear much fruit; so shall ye be my disciples. As the Father hath loved me, so have I loved you: continue ye in my love. If ye keep my commandments, ye shall abide in my love; even as I have kept my Father's commandments, and abide in his love.* John 15:7-10

Perhaps, then, you might hear this solemn warning:

> *If a man abide not in me, he is cast forth as a branch, and is withered; and men gather them into the fire, and they are burned.* John 15:6

My friends, please abide in the Vine. Please get the Word of God deep into you through obedience to it.

It is the Word of God quickened to us by the Holy Spirit that will speak to us. We will be reminded of certain scriptures as we walk day by day, our hand in His. The Scriptures will speak to us, as they guide us along the Way of Righteousness:

> *My son, keep thy father's commandment, and forsake not the law of thy mother: bind them continually upon thine heart, and tie them about thy neck. When thou goest, it shall lead thee; when thou sleepest, it shall keep thee; and when thou awakest, it shall talk with thee. For the commandment is a lamp; and the law is light; and reproofs of instruction are the way of life.* Proverbs 6:20-23

The Classic Edition of the Amplified Bible reads:

> *My son, keep your father's [God-given] commandment and forsake not the law of [God] your mother [taught you]. Bind them continually upon your heart and tie them about your neck. When you go, they [the words of your parents' God] shall lead you; when you sleep, they shall keep you; and when you waken, they shall talk with you. For the commandment is a lamp,*

Are You Working Out Your Own Salvation?

and the whole teaching [of the law] is light, and
reproofs of discipline are the way of life.
                            Proverbs 6:20-23, AMPC

I previously stated that mature Christians bear
fruit. Bearing fruit is our purpose for existence. Jesus
said that when we bear *"much fruit,"* we glorify the
Father. This is recorded in John 15:

> *Herein is my Father glorified, that ye bear much*
> *fruit; so shall ye be my disciples.*   John 15:8

Now, I have heard many descriptions concerning fruit-bearing. I've heard some say that it's the
fruit of righteousness that is being spoken of in
the Scriptures. I've heard others say that it's the
fruit of the Spirit that is important. Others have
said that it's the souls that you win to the Lord
that's the fruit. All this fruit talk was driving me
bananas (pun intended). When I had considered
it long enough, I came to the conclusion that they
were all right.

Let me endeavor to explain. The seed of righteousness was planted in us by our believing and
confession of the work of the Lord Jesus Christ, as
found in Romans 10:

Bearing Fruit Without Ceasing

That if thou shalt confess with thy mouth the
Lord Jesus, and shalt believe in thine heart that
God hath raised him from the dead, thou shalt
be saved. For with the heart man believeth unto
righteousness; and with the mouth confession
is made unto salvation.   Romans 10:9-10

With proper care this seed grew and began to produce an outward display of that same righteousness,
as we (the ground) yielded to it. The outworking of
that righteousness was blanketed with love, which
enfolds and is the essence of all of the fruit of the
Spirit. As we learned earlier, God is love, and love is
holy. And, I add here, holiness is an outward display
(remember working-out) of imputed righteousness.

Now, we know that fruit carries its own seed
within:

And God said, Let the earth bring forth grass,
the herb yielding seed, and the fruit tree yielding
fruit after his kind, whose seed is in itself, upon
the earth: and it was so.   Genesis 1:11

The bearing of fruit produces seed. The fruit of the
Spirit begins to bloom, as His words are quickened
in us. Seeds of righteousness are produced in us, and

with the inspiration of the Holy Spirit we broadcast the seed that has had its work in us. As we spread the seed enclosed in the fruit of the Spirit, souls are won into the Kingdom of God.

Thus, the fruit that is spoken of here is grown from its seed (the Word of God), working in and through us (earthen vessels). So, the fruit produced from the seed of the Word of God is righteousness, the fruit of the Spirit and new converts coming into the Kingdom.

So, let us abide in Christ and bear much fruit as we do so. Don't fight the process. Just learn to abide vitally united to the Vine, and the fruit will come naturally.

Chapter 11

Are You Applying Your Mind to Knowledge?

Listen [consent and submit] to the words of the wise, and apply your mind to my knowledge; for it will be pleasant if you keep them in your mind [believing them]; your lips will be accustomed to [confessing] them.

Proverbs 22:17-18, AMPC

I want to know God the Father, the Son and the Holy Spirit so much more than I already do. But we can only know Him through a personal relationship with the Holy Spirit and the knowledge of His holy written Word. There must be a deep reverence for the written Word of God. Without having a deep reverence for that Word, we would be fooling ourselves to say that we were submitted to Him and loved Him.

Are You Applying Your Mind to Knowledge?

Reading and studying the Word of God should be a priority in each of our lives. If we didn't read His Word, it could be compared to a wife who never made an effort to know anything about her husband. You would be showing no real interest or love toward Him.

This could also be compared to having a fiancee' who was in another place and you never read his letters or paid any attention to what he wrote to you. How would you know that your bridegroom just opened a bank account for you, if you didn't read his letters? Our actions speak far louder than our words.

There must be a deep reverence for the Holy Spirit. By enjoying communion with the Holy Spirit and reverencing Him, we establish a lifelong blessing. If you don't give reverence to the Holy Ghost, you are not giving reverence to God. The Spirit is not an impersonal force; He is a person, the third person of the Godhead. He leads us, so let's follow Him.

In the time of the early Church, the Spirit was very real in the everyday lives of the disciples:

> *But Peter said, Ananias, why hath Satan filled thine heart to lie to the Holy Ghost, and to keep back part of the price of the land? Whiles it remained, was it not thine own? and after it was*

sold, was it not in thine own power? why hast thou conceived this thing in thine heart? thou hast not lied unto men, but unto God.

Acts 5:3-5

Now when they had gone throughout Phrygia and the region of Galatia, and were forbidden of the Holy Ghost to preach the word in Asia.

Acts 16:6

For as many as are led by the Spirit of God, they are the sons of God. Romans 8:14

The Lord of Hosts loves us so very much, and He desires to be at the center of our lives, in order to infuse the life of His presence into everything we do. I want to be a friend of God, don't you?

Remember, He will have no fellowship with darkness, but He will drive darkness away from us, as we yield to Him and fill ourselves with His Word. Having a healthy respect or reverential fear of God is a vital element in the companionship that God, the Holy Spirit, wishes to share with us.

The Bible tells us that the beginning, just the beginning, of wisdom is the reverent fear of the Lord:

Are You Applying Your Mind to Knowledge?

The reverent and worshipful fear of the Lord is the beginning (the chief and choice part) of Wisdom, and the knowledge of the Holy One is insight and understanding.

Proverbs 9:10, AMPC

I once did a study on the word *wisdom* because of a prophetic word that I received from a man named Jim Sepulvada. He had traveled the world sharing with others the message of the Gospel, with signs and wonders following. The prophetic word, when it is released in a wise manner by the unction of the Holy Ghost, can change nations. The prophetic word that Jim Sepulvada gave me went something like this: "Steve, the Lord says to you, 'As you abide in wisdom, I will be with you in power.' "

Friends, that word was scripturally based and it carried a condition. The condition was that I had to abide in wisdom. After receiving that word, I went deeper into the Word of God, specifically Proverbs, and found wisdom in Christ.

I want to know more and more about Him. You see, with each scripture in the Bible there are many layers of understanding. Level after level can be found as we dig deeper and deeper into His Word, the Bible.

The Bible says that the Lord gives wisdom to the righteous:

> *He layeth up sound wisdom for the righteous:*
> *he is a buckler to them that walk uprightly.*
>
> Proverbs 2:7

The Bible tells us that we are priests and kings to God:

> *And hast made us unto our God kings and*
> *priests: and we shall reign on the earth.*
>
> Revelations 5:10

Now, look at what the Bible tells us about digging into or searching in the Word of God and discovering things hidden by the Lord of Hosts:

> *It is the glory of God to conceal a thing, but the*
> *glory of kings is to search out a thing.*
>
> Proverbs 25:2, AMPC

The deeper I went, digging and probing into the mysteries of the Lord, the better I was getting to know Him. I was developing a relationship with the One Who *is* Wisdom. As He quickened His Word to me by His Spirit, my love and reverence for Him grew more and more.

As I grabbed hold of the foot of the great King of all kings, with my face to the ground, He lifted me higher and higher. Each time I lifted my eyes to Him, my vision became clearer and clearer. I could then begin to see eternity and the love and grace He had extended to me.

At the beginning, I was unable to look into His eyes, as they burned with the fire of the purest love and truth. It seemed, though, that the longer I held Him the easier it became for me to look into His fire-filled eyes:

> *And in the midst of the seven candlesticks one like unto the Son of man, clothed with a garment down to the foot, and girt about the paps with a golden girdle. His head and his hairs were white like wool, as white as snow; and his eyes were as a flame of fire; and his feet like unto fine brass, as if they burned in a furnace; and his voice as the sound of many waters. And he had in his right hand seven stars: and out of his mouth went a sharp twoedged sword: and his countenance was as the sun shineth in his strength.* Revelation 1:13-16

With each new look, I was beginning to understand what Isaiah must have felt as he looked upon my King. Those eyes as flames of fire told me of my need for change and located those areas that needed changing. Willingly, with each new day, I gave Him what needed to be changed.

The goal of searching for wisdom changed my direction too, or, I should say, my motive for the search changed. My ultimate goal was adjusted from seeking God's power to that of becoming the embodiment of Wisdom Himself, in order to display the very image of the Lord Jesus Christ. As my deepest parts change to fit Him, I can say with confidence that He is my Love and my Friend:

> *His mouth is most sweet: yea, he is altogether lovely. This is my beloved, and this is my friend, O daughters of Jerusalem.*
>
> Song of Solomon 5:16

It is much easier to believe a feeling, a thought, a popular saying or interesting story than to believe the literal Word of God. Sure, we can mentally agree with the Word. Many people do that and also call themselves Christians. The real issue is belief. Do we really believe the Bible when we are told that we will speak with new tongues, cast out demons and lay hands on the sick and they will recover or do we just mentally agree with it?

> *And these signs will follow those who believe: In My name they will cast out demons; they will speak with new tongues; they will take up serpents; and if they drink anything deadly, it will by no means hurt them; they will lay hands on the sick, and they will recover.*
>
> Mark 16:17-18

Sometimes we sidestep an issue that makes us aware of our own need for the power of God, in order to excuse ourselves from the need to seek His face. We may even set up elaborate defenses to justify our own powerless gospel, complete with detailed doctrine. We view those walking in the power of God with skepticism and criticism. If that is you, repent! Remember, we know a tree by its fruit. We are wasting our time if we are unwilling to humble ourself before God's Word.

I have heard it said, "You can't teach an old dog new tricks." If you are sincere in your quest for the truth and love of God, you will let yourself be taught. If you think you already know everything, you will learn nothing.

As we look upon God's Word and meditate upon it, we will begin to believe in our heart. The truth is that we must really believe His Word before we see it as a visible reality in our lives. We can't wait to see it before we believe it (that is the way the world believes). We must believe it before we see it.

Before continuing, let me stress that God is looking for fruit in us. The fruit of the Spirit—produced and illustrated by a life of prostrating our Spirit, soul and body to Him and to His Word—should always remain our chief goal:

> *Can two walk together, except they be agreed?*
> Amos 3:3

Let's step back for a moment and consider something. Many who are opposed to the idea of confession make the observation that those using the principle of confession are simply doing what is referred to as "name it and claim it" or as I heard it from a wise instructor, "blab it and grab it." These critics state that people who do this type of confession have reduced God to a helpless individual bound by His Word and unable to do anything outside of our belief system of confession.

Are You Applying Your Mind to Knowledge?

Personally, I don't suggest that you take confession that far. It is important that our faith be in God and His Word and not in our own faith. To put this in perspective is to show the difference between having faith toward God or having faith in our own ability to produce faith. If we have faith toward God, that changes everything. Let us trust God together. He is still omniscient, omnipresent, omnipotent and seated on the throne.

Confessing the Word of God can produce no positive results, if you have no personal relationship with the Lord. Without a heartfelt relationship with God based solely on His grace through Jesus or without our choice of commitment to faithfulness, integrity and love for God and the brethren, confession is reduced to nothing more than vain repetition without any real and lasting blessing. It becomes, as the critics believe it to be, "a type of science of the mind, soulish and, therefore, a fruitless endeavor."

If our confession of faith is in *our* faith rather than faith in the Word of God, if our motives were selfish and self-centered, or if the motive for our confession was defiled by contradicting scriptural ethics, then the critics would be right. There must be congruence between our confession of God's Word and our inner man in order to effectually change things. If

165

our outside man lines up with our inside man, we become an unstoppable force in the hand of God.

Godly confession should be a speaking forth of the Word of God, with gratitude for what the Lord has done for us. In this manner, it is not a mere formula, but rather a feeding of our spirit man. When we feed our spirit, we add to our faith:

> *So then faith cometh by hearing, and hearing by the word of God.*   Romans 10:17

As we begin to speak with purely undefiled and selfless motives, our words are now being filled with power by the Holy Spirit. Because we now believe His Word in our heart, things start happening. Our mind is consistently being renewed by His Word, and we are constantly being cleansed by His spoken Word:

> *And be renewed in the spirit of your mind, and put on the new man, who in the likeness of God has been created in righteousness and holiness of truth.*   Ephesians 4:23-24

> *That he might sanctify it, having cleansed it by the washing of water with the word.*
>   Ephesians 5:26

Are You Applying Your Mind to Knowledge?

You are already clean because of the word which
I have spoken to you. John 15:3

Don't stop sowing the seed just because you reap a harvest. Don't stop sowing the seed of the Word if you see no results right away. Sowing the seed of the Word into your heart is accomplished by speaking the Word of God aloud while walking it out in obedience:

Now the parable is this: The seed is the word of
God. Luke 8:11

When I read this verse, I knew that the Word of God enters the heart by way of speaking it:

And these are the ones by the wayside where
the word is sown. When they hear, Satan comes
immediately and takes away the word that was
sown in their hearts. Mark 4:15

But the ones that fell on the good ground are
those who, having heard the word with a noble
and good heart, keep it and bear fruit with pa-
tience. Luke 8:15

But these are the ones sown on good ground, those who hear the word, accept it, and bear fruit: some thirtyfold, some sixty, and some a hundred.   Mark 4:20

The good man out of the good treasure of his heart brings out that which is good, and the evil man out of the evil treasure of his heart brings out that which is evil, for out of the abundance of the heart, his mouth speaks.   Luke 6:45

As we confess God's Word aloud, speaking what He says concerning us, we begin simply by mentally agreeing with it. We are speaking what He says about us. We hear His Word in our own ears and, at first, it seems that nothing is happening. Although our minds may resist the truths found in the Word of God, we will eventually do more than mentally agree with the Word. We will actually begin to believe it in our heart.

When this happens, the Word begins to transfer from just head or mental agreement to heart belief. We start to sense an inner strength where we once had little or none. Then, a marvelous thing happens. Our lives begin to be built up with an inner treasure of righteousness and all manner of the fruit of the

Spirit. The confession we make starts to come out from our heart and not our head. As our heart faith increases, so does the evidence increase. It is heart faith that makes the difference.

Jesus said this:

> *For assuredly, I say to you, Whoever says to this mountain, Be removed and be cast into the sea, and does not doubt in his heart, but believes that those things he says will be done, he will have whatever he says. Therefore I say to you, Whatever things you ask when you pray, believe that you receive them, and you will have them.*
>
> Mark 11:23-24

The very definition of faith is seen in the Scriptures:

> *Now faith is the substance of things hoped for, the evidence of things not seen.*   Hebrews 11:1

Over time, being in Christ and guided by His Spirit, we speak by the unction of the Spirit and truly believe in our heart that those things we say will come to pass. It is then that we have what we say.

Now, I want to pray for you:

Bearing Fruit Without Ceasing

Heavenly Father,

Because of the principle You have shown me in Your Word concerning the process of vocal confession of Your Word and my desire to walk in obedience to Your Word, I declare and decree that Your will, as expressed in the Scriptures, be fulfilled and completed in my life. Let Your Word, as quickened by Your Spirit, awaken my heart to a deeper revelation of Your Word.

May Your will be done in my life. Your Word reveals Your will, Oh God. Faith confession is not a formula or technique in my life, but rather a principle of Your Word. I know I can totally trust You, God. Knowing Your Word, I am confident that Your Word is trustworthy. Therefore, Your Word will always be the final authority in my life. I base my entire life upon You and Your living Word.

In the name of Jesus,
Amen!

What applies in the Scriptures to the Christ (Jesus of Nazareth) applies to me because I am in Him, and He is in me. As I abide in Him, I will see myself as the Father sees Jesus, according to His living Word, for my life is hid with Jesus, the Christ, in God. I am not Jesus, but I am part of Jesus and I bear His name. The oil of anointing is not upon the Head only, but drips down and applies to His flesh and bone, and that's you and I:

> *For ye are dead, and your life is hid with Christ in God.*   Colossians 3:3

> *It is like the precious ointment upon the head, that ran down upon the beard, even Aaron's beard: that went down to the skirts of his garments.*   Psalm 133:2

> *For we are members of his body, of his flesh, and of his bones.*   Ephesians 5:30

The same things that God says concerning Jesus in His Word apply to me because I am hidden in Christ! I agree with God's Word. Therefore, I believe I have what I say!

> *For verily I say unto you, That whosoever shall say unto this mountain, Be thou removed, and be thou cast into the sea; and*

shall not doubt in his heart, but shall believe that those things which he saith shall come to pass; he shall have whatsoever he saith.

Mark 11:23

The Workout

For God so loved the world, that he gave his
only begotten Son, that whosoever believeth in
him should not perish, but have everlasting life.

John 3:16

I have often heard the Bible referred to as "a love letter from God." I wish to convey this truth in this section by helping to convince us with consistent reminders, that the entire motivation of the Scriptures is based upon His love for us. It is my hope that these self-confessions will help to convince us of the great love God has for us, as it births revelation of this fact in us.

In this section, I will start by reading at least one scriptural promise. After reading that scripture or scriptures, I will be making a statement of conclusion which summarizes the meaning as it applies to the life of a believer, and an affirmation of the love of God will be included in it. Place your eyes upon the scriptures and read them aloud in order to hear God's Word in your ears. Follow along and repeat the conclusion after having heard it once. Doing this will get your journey of blessings started today!

Let us begin.

John 3:16[1]

> *For God so loved the world that He gave His only begotten Son, that whoever believes in Him should not perish but have everlasting life.*

John 10:11

> *I am the good shepherd. The good shepherd gives His life for the sheep.*

Conclusion: The Lord God of Heaven and Earth and His Son, the Lord Jesus Christ, LOVE ME. I know this because God sent His Son, Who laid down His life for me.

෨

Romans 6:23

> *For the wages of sin is death, but the gift of God is eternal life in Christ Jesus our Lord.*

---

1. All verses used in the Workout are from the New King James Version of the Bible, see the copyright page for rights details.

The Workout

John 3:15-16

> *That whoever believes in Him should not perish but have eternal life. For God so loved the world that He gave His only begotten Son, that whoever believes in him should not perish but have everlasting life.*

Conclusion: God loves me. I know this because He gave me the gift of eternal life in Heaven, bringing me to belief and trust in Jesus.

હ

2 Corinthians 5:17

> *Therefore, if anyone is in Christ, he is a new creation; old things have passed away; behold, all things have become new.*

Conclusion: He loves me. I know this because my old life is gone. He made me a new creation!

હ

1 Peter 1:23

> *Having been born again, not of corruptible seed but incorruptible, through the word of God which lives and abides forever.*

175

Conclusion: He loves me! I know this because He caused me to be born again!

∞

Ephesians 2:4-6

> *But God, who is rich in mercy, because of His great love with which He loved us, even when we were dead in trespasses, made us alive together with Christ (by grace you have been saved), and raised us up together, and made us sit together in the heavenly places in Christ Jesus.*

Conclusion: God loves me. I know this because He placed me together with Christ at His right hand.

∞

1 Corinthians 16:22

> *If anyone does not love the Lord Jesus Christ, let him be accursed.*

2 Corinthians 2:8

> *Therefore I urge you to reaffirm your love to him.*

The Workout

1 John 4:19

We love Him because He first loved us.

Psalm 119:160

The entirety of Your word is truth,
And every one of Your righteous judgments
endures forever.

John 17:17

Sanctify them by Your truth. Your word is
truth.

Conclusion: Jesus loves me, and I love Him. I know this is true. I am sanctified by His Word. His Word is truth.

೮೦

2 Corinthians 5:21

For He made Him who knew no sin to be sin
for us, that we might become the righteousness
of God in Him.

Conclusion: He loves me and this is demonstrated by the fact that He made me the righteousness of God in Christ Jesus.

೮೦

2 Timothy 2:13

If we are faithless, He remains faithful; He cannot deny Himself.

Conclusion: He loves me and this is proven by His faithfulness to me.

෨

Habakkuk 3:19

The LORD God is my strength;
He will make my feet like deer's feet,
And He will make me walk on my high hills.

Conclusion: The Lord loves me. He gives me strength and keeps my feet from slipping.

෨

Proverbs 15:29

The LORD is far from the wicked,
But He hears the prayer of the righteous.

1 John 5:14

Now this is the confidence that we have in Him,
that if we ask anything according to His will,
He hears us.

The Workout

John 15:7

> *If you abide in Me, and My words abide in you, you will ask what you desire, and it shall be done for you.*

Conclusion: He loves me, and this is shown by the fact that He answers my prayers.

&

John 10:14

> *I am the good shepherd; and I know My sheep, and am known by My own.*

John 10:27

> *My sheep hear My voice, and I know them, and they follow Me.*

Conclusion: He loves me. I know this because He made me one of His sheep. I hear His voice, so I follow Him, and I know that He knows me.

&

Galatians 3:26

> *For you are all sons of God through faith in Christ Jesus.*

Romans 8:14

> *For as many as are led by the Spirit of God, these are sons of God.*

Conclusion: He loves me. I know this because He made me a son of God, and that is why I follow Him.

જી

1 Corinthians 1:9

> *God is faithful, by whom you were called into the fellowship of His Son, Jesus Christ our Lord.*

Conclusion: He loves me and this is shown by His fellowship with me.

જી

Hebrews 12:7

> *If you endure chastening, God deals with you as with sons; for what son is there whom a father does not chasten?*

Conclusion: He loves me and this is demonstrated by the fact that He corrects me when I get off the path of righteousness.

જી

The Workout

John 14:6

> *Jesus said to him, "I am the way, the truth, and the life. No one comes to the Father except through Me."*

John 15:4

> *Abide in Me, and I in you. As the branch cannot bear fruit of itself, unless it abides in the vine, neither can you, unless you abide in Me.*

Conclusion: He loves me so much that He desires for me to abide in truth always.

ၹ

1 Peter 5:7

> *Casting all your care upon Him, for He cares for you.*

Conclusion: He loves me and shows His love by caring for what I care about.

ၹ

2 Peter 3:9

> *The Lord is not slack concerning His promise, as some count slackness, but is longsuffering*

toward us, not willing that any should perish but that all should come to repentance.

Psalm 18:30

As for God, His way is perfect;
The word of the LORD is proven;
He is a shield to all who trust in Him.

Conclusion: He loves me and takes actions that illustrate that love.

৪০

Psalm 91:14

Because he has set his love upon Me, therefore
I will deliver him;
I will set him on high, because he has known
My name.

2 Thessalonians 3:3

But the Lord is faithful, who will establish you
and guard you from the evil one.

Conclusion: He loves me and this is shown by the fact that He raises me up to a place of safety, protecting me and delivering me from all harm.

৪০

The Workout

Psalm 103:3

Who forgives all your iniquities,
Who heals all your diseases.

Psalm 147:3

He heals the brokenhearted
And binds up their wounds.

Isaiah 53:5

But He was wounded for our transgressions,
He was bruised for our iniquities;
The chastisement for our peace was upon Him,
And by His stripes we are healed.

1 Peter 2:24

Who Himself bore our sins in His own body on the tree, that we, having died to sins, might live for righteousness—by whose stripes you were healed.

Exodus 23:25-26

So you shall serve the LORD your God, and He will bless your bread and your water. And I will take sickness away from the midst of you. No one shall suffer miscarriage or be barren in your land; I will fulfill the number of your days.

Proverbs 4:20-22

> *My son, give attention to my words;*
> *Incline your ear to my sayings.*
> *Do not let them depart from your eyes;*
> *Keep them in the midst of your heart;*
> *for they are life to those who find them,*
> *And health to all their flesh.*

Conclusion: He loves me and this is shown by the fact that He cures me of any sickness or problem in my body and prevents sickness in my body. The Lord blesses my bread and water and my family with fruitfulness. Because I take heed to the Word of God and study it, I have good health and will enjoy long life, fulfilling my days.

෨

1 Peter 5:7

> *Casting all your care upon Him, for He cares*
> *for you.*

Conclusion: He loves me and this is shown by His love for my children, as I give them to Him.

෨

The Workout

1 Corinthians 1:24

But to those who are called, both Jews and Greeks, Christ the power of God and the wisdom of God.

Conclusion: He loves me. I know this because He has given me the very power and wisdom of God.

෨

Proverbs 13:22

A good man leaves an inheritance to his children's children,
But the wealth of the sinner is stored up for the righteous.

Proverbs 8:21 (speaking of wisdom)

That I may cause those who love me to inherit wealth,
That I may fill their treasuries.

Psalm 72:15

And He shall live;
And the gold of Sheba will be given to Him;
Prayer also will be made for Him continually,
And daily He shall be praised.

Philippians 4:19

> *And my God shall supply all your need according to His riches in glory by Christ Jesus.*

Conclusion: He loves me and this is demonstrated in the great provision He supplies for me and the wealth He transfers to me.

ಀ

1 John 4:7

> *Beloved, let us love one another, for love is of God; and everyone who loves is born of God and knows God.*

Conclusion: He loves me because this is His nature. He loves me, I love Him, and, because He is in me, I love others.

ಀ

John 15:9

> *As the Father loved Me, I also have loved you; abide in My love.*

Conclusion: He loves me. Therefore I abide in His love.

ಀ

The Workout

1 Thessalonians 3:12

And may the Lord make you increase and abound in love to one another and to all, just as we do to you,

Ephesians 1:17-19

That the God of our Lord Jesus Christ, the Father of glory, may give to you the spirit of wisdom and revelation in the knowledge of Him, the eyes of your understanding being enlightened; that you may know what is the hope of His calling, what are the riches of the glory of His inheritance in the saints, and what is the exceeding greatness of His power toward us who believe, according to the working of His mighty power

Conclusion: God loves me and I know this because He gives me the revelation of how very much He loves me. He opens my eyes and touches my heart and my spirit with the realization of the fact that He loves me and, because of Him, I love other people.

80

Psalm 17:8

> *Keep me as the apple of Your eye;*
> *Hide me under the shadow of Your wings,*

Conclusion: He loves me. I know that He loves me because I am the apple of His eye.

ॐ

Romans 8:38-39

> *For I am persuaded that neither death nor life,*
> *nor angels nor principalities nor powers, nor*
> *things present nor things to come, nor height*
> *nor depth, nor any other created thing, shall be*
> *able to separate us from the love of God which*
> *is in Christ Jesus our Lord.*

Conclusion: I know that God loves me because nothing can separate me from His love in Christ.

ॐ

1 John 2:5

> *But whoever keeps His word, truly the love of*
> *God is perfected in him. By this we know that*
> *we are in Him.*

The Workout

John 14:15

> *If you love Me, keep My commandments.*

Conclusion: I know that He loves me because I abide in the love of Jesus and do what He said for me to do.

ဆာ

James 1:22

> *But be doers of the word, and not hearers only, deceiving yourselves.*

Conclusion: He loves me, and therefore, I am a doer of His Word.

ဆာ

Mark 11:23

> *For assuredly, I say to you, whoever says to this mountain, "Be removed and be cast into the sea," and does not doubt in his heart, but believes that those things he says will be done, he will have whatever he says.*

Conclusion: I know God loves me, for I have what I say!

ဆာ

Romans 10:8-10

But what does it say? "The word is near you, in your mouth and in your heart" (that is, the word of faith which we preach): that if you confess with your mouth the Lord Jesus and believe in your heart that God has raised Him from the dead, you will be saved. For with the heart one believes unto righteousness, and with the mouth confession is made unto salvation. For the Scripture says, "Whoever believes on Him will not be put to shame."

Conclusion: He loves me. Because I confess with my lips that Jesus is Lord and believe in my heart that God raised Him from the dead, I am justified and made righteous, and my salvation is confirmed.

હ

Deuteronomy 6:5

You shall love the LORD your God with all your heart, with all your soul, and with all your strength.

Leviticus 19:18

You shall not take vengeance, nor bear any grudge against the children of your people, but you shall love your neighbor as yourself: I am the LORD.

Conclusion: I love the Lord God with all my heart, with all my soul and with all my strength, and therefore I love my neighbor as myself

ଈଞ

Ephesians 2:13

But now in Christ Jesus you who once were far off have been brought near by the blood of Christ.

Conclusion: God loves me and draws me near to Himself through the blood of Christ.

ଈଞ

1 Corinthians 6:11

And such were some of you. But you were washed, but you were sanctified, but you were justified in the name of the Lord Jesus and by the Spirit of our God.

Conclusion: He loves me, and I know this because He washed, sanctified and justified me in the name of Jesus and through His Spirit.

Psalm 103:12

As far as the east is from the west,
So far has He removed our transgressions from
us.

Conclusion: He loves me and I know this because He caused my sins to be washed away and removed from me as far as the east is from the west.

ℬ

Romans 6:11

Likewise you also, reckon yourselves to be dead
indeed to sin, but alive to God in Christ Jesus
our Lord.

Conclusion: He loves me and I know this because He makes me dead to sin and alive unto Him.

ℬ

Romans 12:1

I beseech you therefore, brethren, by the mercies
of God, that you present your bodies a living
sacrifice, holy, acceptable to God, which is your
reasonable service.

The Workout

Conclusion: I love Him and I make a continuing decision of dedication to Him by giving my body to Him daily, for this is my reasonable service and act of worship in response to His love.

బ

Galatians 3:13

Christ has redeemed us from the curse of the law, having become a curse for us (for it is written, "Cursed is everyone who hangs on a tree").

Conclusion: God loves me. I know this because He redeemed me from the curse of the Law.

బ

John 6:63

It is the Spirit who gives life; the flesh profits nothing. The words that I speak to you are spirit, and they are life.

John 10:4

And when he brings out his own sheep, he goes before them; and the sheep follow him, for they know his voice.

Conclusion: He loves me and I know His voice. He gave me life when I heard His Spirit-filled Word.

∞

Romans 8:2

For the law of the Spirit of life in Christ Jesus has made me free from the law of sin and death.

Conclusion: He loves me. I know this because He made me free from the Law of sin and death.

∞

Romans 8:1

There is therefore now no condemnation to those who are in Christ Jesus, who do not walk according to the flesh, but according to the Spirit.

Conclusion: I love Jesus. Therefore, I experience no condemnation.

∞

John 8:31-32

Then Jesus said to those Jews who believed Him, "If you abide in My word, you are My disciples indeed. And you shall know the truth, and the truth shall make you free."

The Workout

Romans 5:5

Now hope does not disappoint, because the love of God has been poured out in our hearts by the Holy Spirit who was given to us.

Psalm 4:5

Offer the sacrifices of righteousness,
And put your trust in the LORD.

Psalm 5:11

But let all those rejoice who put their trust in You;
Let them ever shout for joy, because You defend them;
Let those also who love Your name
Be joyful in You.

2 Corinthians 1:9

Yes, we had the sentence of death in ourselves, that we should not trust in ourselves but in God who raises the dead,

Deuteronomy 31:6

Be strong and of good courage, do not fear nor be afraid of them; for the LORD your God, He is the One who goes with you. He will not leave you nor forsake you."

Hebrews 13:5

Let your conduct be without covetousness; be content with such things as you have. For He Himself has said, "I will never leave you nor forsake you."

Conclusion: He loves me and I know this because I have been set free. He made me free to love and to trust Him without fear of rejection or of being hurt.

ॐ

John 8:12

Then Jesus spoke to them again, saying, "I am the light of the world. He who follows Me shall not walk in darkness, but have the light of life."

Conclusion: I love Jesus and follow Him. He gave me the Light of Life.

ॐ

Psalm 104:1-2

Bless the LORD, O my soul!
O LORD my God, You are very great:

The Workout

You are clothed with honor and majesty,
Who cover Yourself with light as with a gar-
ment,
Who stretch out the heavens like a curtain.

Matthew 5:14

You are the light of the world. A city that is set
on a hill cannot be hidden.

Conclusion: I love the Lord Jesus. He covers Himself
with light as a garment and, in like manner, He
covers and fills me with the armor of His light and
has made me a light to the world.

ஒ

John 10:10

The thief does not come except to steal, and
to kill, and to destroy. I have come that they
may have life, and that they may have it more
abundantly.

Conclusion: God loves me and has given me abun-
dant life.

ஒ

Galatians 4:7

> *Therefore you are no longer a slave but a son, and if a son, then an heir of God through Christ.*

Romans 8:29

> *For whom He foreknew, He also predestined to be conformed to the image of His Son, that He might be the firstborn among many brethren.*

Conclusion: God loves me and has made me His son (or daughter) and heir.

જી

Ephesians 1:13

> *In Him you also trusted, after you heard the word of truth, the gospel of your salvation; in whom also, having believed, you were sealed with the Holy Spirit of promise.*

Conclusion: He loves me. I heard the Word of truth and believed, and I am sealed with the Holy Spirit because of it.

જી

The Workout

Romans 7:4

Therefore, my brethren, you also have become dead to the law through the body of Christ, that you may be married to another — to Him who was raised from the dead, that we should bear fruit to God.

Conclusion: God loves me. He married me to Christ in order to bring forth good fruit from my life.

ॐ

2 Timothy 2:15

Study to shew thyself approved unto God, a workman that needeth not to be ashamed, rightly dividing the word of truth.

Psalm 89:22

The enemy shall not outwit him,
Nor the son of wickedness afflict him.

Conclusion: God loves me and that is why I study the Bible and quickly catch the devil in all of his deceitful lies.

ॐ

2 Corinthians 10:3-5

For though we walk in the flesh, we do not war according to the flesh. For the weapons of our warfare are not carnal but mighty in God for pulling down strongholds, casting down arguments and every high thing that exalts itself against the knowledge of God, bringing every thought into captivity to the obedience of Christ.

Conclusion: He loves me. I take every thought captive unto the obedience of Jesus Christ, casting down every imagination and every high and lofty thing that exalts itself against the knowledge of God.

John 15:9-10

As the Father loved Me, I also have loved you; abide in My love. If you keep My commandments, you will abide in My love, just as I have kept My Father's commandments and abide in His love.

1 John 2:5

But whoever keeps His word, truly the love of God is perfected in him. By this we know that we are in Him.

The Workout

Conclusion: God loves me. As I learn to treasure and abide in the love of God, keeping His Word, His love is perfected in me, and I know I am in Him.

ဆာ

Philippians 1:6

> *Being confident of this very thing, that He who has begun a good work in you will complete it until the day of Jesus Christ.*

Conclusion: He loves me. I know this because His plans and purposes in my life are established and carried out.

ဆာ

Philippians 4:13

> *I can do all things through Christ who strengthens me.*

John 5:19

> *Then Jesus answered and said to them, "Most assuredly, I say to you, the Son can do nothing of Himself, but what He sees the Father do; for whatever He does, the Son also does in like manner."*

John 15:5

I am the vine, you are the branches. He who abides in Me, and I in him, bears much fruit; for without Me you can do nothing.

Conclusion: I know Jesus loves me. Because I do as I see our Father do, there is nothing I cannot do with Him on my side.

ഇ

John 14:12

"Most assuredly, I say to you, he who believes in Me, the works that I do he will do also; and greater works than these he will do, because I go to My Father."

Conclusion: I love Jesus and I operate in all the gifts of the Holy Spirit.

ഇ

Romans 7:4

Therefore, my brethren, you also have become dead to the law through the body of Christ, that you may be married to another — to Him who was raised from the dead, that we should bear fruit to God.

The Workout

Galatians 5:22-23

> *But the fruit of the Spirit is love, joy, peace, longsuffering, kindness, goodness, faithfulness, gentleness, self-control. Against such there is no law.*

Mark 11:24

> *Therefore I say to you, whatever things you ask when you pray, believe that you receive them, and you will have them.*

John 15:5

> *I am the vine, you are the branches. He who abides in Me, and I in him, bears much fruit; for without Me you can do nothing.*

Conclusion: Because I love Jesus, I bear the fruit of the Spirit.

જ

Hebrews 10:19-20

> *Therefore, brethren, having boldness to enter the Holiest by the blood of Jesus, by a new and living way which He consecrated for us, through the veil, that is, His flesh ... .*

Conclusion: God loves me and by the power and virtue of the blood of Jesus, I now can enter the Holy of Holies with confidence.

છ

John 6:35

And Jesus said to them, "I am the bread of life. He who comes to Me shall never hunger, and he who believes in Me shall never thirst."

Colossians 2:9-10

For in Him dwells all the fullness of the God-head bodily; and you are complete in Him, who is the head of all principality and power.

Conclusion: He loves me, and I am filled with His Word and life because I am filled with the fullness of the Godhead—Father, Son and Holy Spirit.

છ

Ephesians 3:19

To know the love of Christ which passes knowl-edge; that you may be filled with all the fullness of God.

The Workout

Conclusion: I know the love of Christ and am filled with the fullness of God.

ॐ

1 Peter 2:9

> *But you are a chosen generation, a royal priesthood, a holy nation, His own special people, that you may proclaim the praises of Him who called you out of darkness into His marvelous light.*

Conclusion: Because God loves me, He made me part of a royal priesthood.

ॐ

1 John 5:20

> *And we know that the Son of God has come and has given us an understanding, that we may know Him who is true; and we are in Him who is true, in His Son Jesus Christ. This is the true God and eternal life.*

Conclusion: God loves me and has given me understanding and insight to progressively get to know Him Who is Life eternal—Jesus Christ.

ॐ

Revelation 1:8

"I am the Alpha and the Omega, the Beginning and the End," says the Lord, "who is and who was and who is to come, the Almighty."

Revelation 1:17

And when I saw Him, I fell at His feet as dead. But He laid His right hand on me, saying to me, "Do not be afraid; I am the First and the Last."

John 14:23

Jesus answered and said to him, "If anyone loves Me, he will keep My word; and My Father will love him, and We will come to him and make Our home with him.

1 Corinthians 6:19

Or do you not know that your body is the temple of the Holy Spirit who is in you, whom you have from God, and you are not your own?

1 Corinthians 3:17

If anyone defiles the temple of God, God will destroy him. For the temple of God is holy, which temple you are.

The Workout

Conclusion: The Lord of Hosts, the Sovereign God and Father of all, the One Who is the Alpha and Omega, the Beginning and the End, the First and the Last, Who was and is and is to come the Almighty, loves me and is living within me, His temple. Therefore, I keep myself clean and undefiled.

છ

Isaiah 54:10

> *For the mountains shall depart*
> *And the hills be removed,*
> *But My kindness shall not depart from you,*
> *Nor shall My covenant of peace be removed,"*
> *Says the LORD, who has mercy on you.*

Conclusion: Because the Lord loves me, His kindness and covenant of peace with me shall never be removed.

છ

Romans 8:14

> *For as many as are led by the Spirit of God, these*
> *are sons of God.*

Conclusion: He loves me. I walk in the Spirit and am led by the Spirit at all times.

છે

Psalm 91:11

> *For He shall give His angels charge over you,*
> *to keep you in all your ways.*

Conclusion: God loves me and that is why His angels protect me and go with me, preparing the way before me.

છે

Hebrews 1:14

> *Are they not all ministering spirits sent forth*
> *to minister for those who will inherit salvation?*

Conclusion: He loves me and I know this because He sends ministering angels to work with me.

છે

2 Kings 6:16

> *So he answered, "Do not fear, for those who*
> *are with us are more than those who are with*
> *them."*

The Workout

Conclusion: The Lord God loves me and I know this because He assigns huge warring angels to be by my side, protecting me. The army of the Lord of Hosts accompanies me.

৯০

Psalm 105:14-15

> *He permitted no one to do them wrong;*
> *Yes, He rebuked kings for their sakes,*
> *Saying, "Do not touch My anointed ones,*
> *And do My prophets no harm."*

Conclusion: Because He loves me, the Lord permits no one to do me wrong. He rebukes kings for my sake. The Lord speaks to the kings of the earth concerning me, "Touch not My anointed; neither do My prophet any harm."

Proverbs 3:24

> *When you lie down, you will not be afraid;*
> *Yes, you will lie down and your sleep will be sweet.*

Conclusion: Because God loves me, He does not allow fear to touch me, and my sleep is sweet.

৯০

Hebrews 13:5-6

Let your conduct be without covetousness; be content with such things as you have. For He Himself has said, "I will never leave you nor forsake you." So we may boldly say:
"The Lord is my helper;
I will not fear.
What can man do to me?"

Conclusion: Because Jesus loves me, He will never leave me. I can say that He is my help, and I will not fear man.

ജ

1 Peter 5:6-7

Therefore humble yourselves under the mighty hand of God, that He may exalt you in due time, casting all your care upon Him, for He cares for you.

Conclusion: I humble myself before God, casting all worries to Him, because He affectionately cares for me and, as a result, I don't have to worry about anything. He also exalts me in the proper season.

ജ

The Workout

Philippians 4:8

> *Finally, brethren, whatever things are true, whatever things are noble, whatever things are just, whatever things are pure, whatever things are lovely, whatever things are of good report, if there is any virtue and if there is anything praiseworthy—meditate on these things.*

Conclusion: Because I love the Lord, I choose to obey His Word and think on what is true, noble, just, pure, lovely, and of good report, as well as virtuous and praiseworthy.

තු

John 10:14

> *I am the good shepherd; and I know My sheep, and am known by My own.*

John 10:27

> *My sheep hear My voice, and I know them, and they follow Me.*

Isaiah 30:21

> *Your ears shall hear a word behind you, saying, "This is the way, walk in it,"*

*Whenever you turn to the right hand
Or whenever you turn to the left.*

John 14:10

*Do you not believe that I am in the Father, and
the Father in Me? The words that I speak to
you I do not speak on My own authority; but
the Father who dwells in Me does the works.*

John 6:63

*It is the Spirit who gives life; the flesh profits
nothing. The words that I speak to you are
spirit, and they are life.*

Conclusion: I have ears to hear and I hear the voice
of the Lord. Because the Lord lives within me and
loves me, I am led by His Spirit in what I say. I
speak the words He gives me to speak, and He
brings to pass all that I say. My words are spirit
and life to all who hear them.

෨

James 3:10-12

*Out of the same mouth proceed blessing and
cursing. My brethren, these things ought not to
be so. Does a spring send forth fresh water and*

The Workout

bitter from the same opening? Can a fig tree, my brethren, bear olives, or a grapevine bear figs? Thus no spring yields both salt water and fresh.

Conclusion: Because I love the Lord and love other people, I will use my tongue to speak blessings today and every day.

෨

Psalm 141:3

*Set a guard, O Lord, over my mouth;
Keep watch over the door of my lips.*

Hebrews 10:9

Then He said, "Behold, I have come to do Your will, O God." He takes away the first that He may establish the second.

Conclusion: Because God loves me, He helps me to guard my tongue and speak according to His will today and every day.

෨

Colossians 4:5-6

Walk in wisdom toward those who are outside, redeeming the time. Let your speech always be with grace, seasoned with salt, that you may know how you ought to answer each one.

Conclusion: Jesus loves me and helps me to make my conversation full of grace and seasoned with salt, so that I may give a good reason for my faith.

℘

Matthew 3:11

I indeed baptize you with water unto repentance, but He who is coming after me is mightier than I, whose sandals I am not worthy to carry. He will baptize you with the Holy Spirit and fire.

Conclusion: Because Jesus loves me, He baptized me with the Holy Ghost and fire.

℘

Ephesians 1:3

Blessed be the God and Father of our Lord Jesus Christ, who has blessed us with every spiritual blessing in the heavenly places in Christ.

Conclusion: The Lord loves me. I am blessed with all spiritual blessings in heavenly places.

℘

The Workout

Proverbs 28:1

The wicked flee when no one pursues,
But the righteous are bold as a lion.

Matthew 10:16

Behold, I send you out as sheep in the midst
of wolves. Therefore be wise as serpents and
harmless as doves.

Conclusion: Jesus loves me and gives me His wisdom. He makes me to be as bold as a lion and as gentle as a dove.

ജ

1 Peter 2:6

Therefore it is also contained in the Scripture,
"Behold, I lay in Zion
A chief cornerstone, elect, precious,
And he who believes on Him will by no means
be put to shame."

Conclusion: Because the Lord loves me, He never allows me to be put to shame.

ജ

2 Corinthians 5:17

Therefore, if anyone is in Christ, he is a new creation; old things have passed away; behold, all things have become new.

Conclusion: Because the Lord loves me, He has made me a new creation and has given me a fresh start in life.

જી

Colossians 3:3

For you died, and your life is hidden with Christ in God.

Conclusion: Because God loves me, He has hidden my life with Christ in Himself.

જી

Ephesians 6:13-17

Therefore take up the whole armor of God, that you may be able to withstand in the evil day, and having done all, to stand. Stand therefore, having girded your waist with truth, having put on the breastplate of righteousness, and having shod your feet with the preparation of the gospel of peace; above all, taking the shield of faith with which you will be able to quench all the fiery darts of the wicked one. And take the helmet of salvation, and the sword of the Spirit, which is the word of God;

Conclusion: God loves me and has made me able to stand in the evil day, because I have His whole armor upon me and the sword of the Spirit in my hand.

℘

John 10:27

My sheep hear My voice, and I know them, and they follow Me.

Conclusion: Because God loves me, He made me to know His voice, and I always obey what He tells me.

℘

John 16:13

However, when He, the Spirit of truth, has come, He will guide you into all truth; for He will not speak on His own authority, but whatever He hears He will speak; and He will tell you things to come.

Conclusion: Because He loves me, the Holy Spirit within and upon me guides me into the full truth and repeats to me what He hears at the throne of the Father. He also shows me things before they happen.

෨

John 5:19-20

Then Jesus answered and said to them, "Most assuredly, I say to you, the Son can do nothing of Himself, but what He sees the Father do; for whatever He does, the Son also does in like manner. For the Father loves the Son, and shows Him all things that He Himself does; and He will show Him greater works than these, that you may marvel."

Conclusion: Because He loves me, the Holy Spirit shows me what the Father is doing, so that I may do as He does, just as Jesus did what He saw the Father doing.

෨

Acts 10:38

How God anointed Jesus of Nazareth with the Holy Spirit and with power, who went about

The Workout

doing good and healing all who were oppressed by the devil, for God was with Him.

John 20:21

So Jesus said to them again, "Peace to you! As the Father has sent Me, I also send you."

Psalm 71:16

I will go in the strength of the LORD God; I will make mention of Your righteousness, of Yours only.

Matthew 28:19

Go therefore and make disciples of all the nations, baptizing them in the name of the Father and of the Son and of the Holy Spirit.

Conclusion: Because Jesus loves me, He sends me to the nations in the strength of the Lord, speaking His Word of righteousness, going about doing good, healing all who are oppressed by the devil, making disciples, teaching and baptizing them in the name of the Father, the Son and the Holy Ghost.

॰

John 16:8-11

> *And when He has come, He will convict the world of sin, and of righteousness, and of judgment: of sin, because they do not believe in Me; of righteousness, because I go to My Father and you see Me no more; of judgment, because the ruler of this world is judged.*

Conclusion: Because God loves me, as I preach the Word of righteousness, the Holy Spirit convicts, convinces and brings demonstration about sin, righteousness and judgment, by helping to convince and convict the people of the truth, along with the demonstration of the destruction of the works of the devil, with signs and wonders, to further convince them.

ଚଚ

Acts 4:29-30

> *Now, Lord, look on their threats, and grant to Your servants that with all boldness they may speak Your word, by stretching out Your hand to heal, and that signs and wonders may be done through the name of Your holy Servant Jesus.*

The Workout

1 John 5:15

> *And if we know that He hears us, whatever we ask, we know that we have the petitions that we have asked of Him.*

Conclusion: Because He loves me, God hears my prayers and gives me my requests and grants boldness to me while I'm preaching the Word of righteousness, with signs and wonders that confirm His Word. I have what I say!

છે

John 14:12

> *Most assuredly, I say to you, he who believes in Me, the works that I do he will do also; and greater works than these he will do, because I go to My Father.*

Isaiah 35:5-6

> *Then the eyes of the blind shall be opened,*
> *And the ears of the deaf shall be unstopped.*
> *Then the lame shall leap like a deer,*
> *And the tongue of the dumb sing.*
> *For waters shall burst forth in the wilderness,*
> *And streams in the desert.*

Conclusion: Because God loves me and I steadfastly believe and rely upon Jesus, as I go, I pray for the blind, and their eyes are opened; I pray for the lame, and they are able to run like a deer; I pray for the dumb, and they can sing joyously; I pray for the deaf, and their ears are opened. An endless supply of the Spirit of God flows abundantly through me.

ജ

2 Corinthians 2:14-15

Now thanks be to God who always leads us in triumph in Christ, and through us diffuses the fragrance of His knowledge in every place. For we are to God the fragrance of Christ among those who are being saved and among those who are perishing.

Conclusion: Because God loves me, He has made me a trophy of the victory of Christ. I am the sweet fragrance of Christ and of the knowledge of God, and, as this knowledge is spread abroad, this fragrance is noticed by everyone.

ജ

The Workout

2 Corinthians 5:18

Now all things are of God, who has reconciled us to Himself through Jesus Christ, and has given us the ministry of reconciliation,

Conclusion: Because God loves me, He has reconciled me to Himself by Jesus Christ and has given me the ministry of reconciliation.

❧

Philippians 4:13

I can do all things through Christ who strengthens me.

Conclusion: Because God loves me, I can face any challenge with the strength that comes from Christ.

❧

2 Timothy 1:7

For God has not given us a spirit of fear, but of power and of love and of a sound mind.

1 Corinthians 2:16

For "who has known the mind of the Lord that he may instruct Him?" But we have the mind of Christ.

Conclusion: Because the Lord loves me, He has given me power, love and a sound mind. I have the mind of Christ.

૪૭

Joel 2:28-30

And it shall come to pass afterward
That I will pour out My Spirit on all flesh;
Your sons and your daughters shall prophesy,
Your old men shall dream dreams,
Your young men shall see visions.
And also on My menservants and on My maid-
servants
I will pour out My Spirit in those days.
And I will show wonders in the heavens and in
the earth:
Blood and fire and pillars of smoke.

Proverbs 1:23

Turn at my rebuke;
Surely I will pour out my spirit on you;
I will make my words known to you.

1 Corinthians 14:29

Let two or three prophets speak, and let the oth-
ers judge.

The Workout

Conclusion: Because God loves me, He gives me prophecy, dreams and visions and a clear interpretation of them for myself and others. He has also given me wisdom to judge all prophecy properly and accurately by the Holy Spirit.

೫

Psalm 46:10

Be still, and know that I am God:
I will be exalted among the heathen,
I will be exalted in the earth.

Conclusion: I love the Lord, so I will be still and watch how He exalts Himself and shows forth His mighty power to honor His Word through me. I am His heritage, His inheritance, and He is my Refuge. The Lord blesses His inheritance.

೫

Psalm 5:12

For You, O Lord, will bless the righteous;
With favor You will surround him as with a
shield.

Psalm 89:17

> *For You are the glory of their strength,*
> *And in Your favor our horn is exalted.*

Proverbs 3:3-4

> *Let not mercy and truth forsake you;*
> *Bind them around your neck,*
> *Write them on the tablet of your heart,*
> *And so find favor and high esteem*
> *In the sight of God and man.*

Proverbs 8:35

> *For whoever finds me finds life,*
> *And obtains favor from the* LORD;

Psalm 112:9

> *He has dispersed abroad,*
> *He has given to the poor;*
> *His righteousness endures forever;*
> *His horn will be exalted with honor.*

Conclusion: I am given favor with God and man. God honors me and surrounds me with His favor.

ଛ

The Workout

Proverbs 4:8

> *Exalt her, and she will promote you;*
> *She will bring you honor, when you embrace her.*

Psalm 71:21

> *You shall increase my greatness,*
> *And comfort me on every side.*

Conclusion: Jesus is my wisdom. Because I love Him and embrace the wisdom of God, He promotes me and brings me honor.

෨

Isaiah 54:15-17

> *Indeed they shall surely assemble, but not because of Me.*
> *Whoever assembles against you shall fall for your sake.*
> *"Behold, I have created the blacksmith*
> *Who blows the coals in the fire,*
> *Who brings forth an instrument for his work;*
> *And I have created the spoiler to destroy.*
> *No weapon formed against you shall prosper,*
> *And every tongue which rises against you in judgment*

You shall condemn.
This is the heritage of the servants of the LORD,
And their righteousness is from Me,"
Says the LORD.

Conclusion: The Lord loves me, gives me His righteousness and causes those who conspire against me to fall. No weapon formed from the arsenal of the enemy is successful against me, and every tongue that speaks against me is condemned.

৯০

Mark 16:17-18

And these signs will follow those who believe: In My name they will cast out demons; they will speak with new tongues; they will take up serpents; and if they drink anything deadly, it will by no means hurt them; they will lay hands on the sick, and they will recover.

Luke 10:19

Behold, I give you the authority to trample on serpents and scorpions, and over all the power of the enemy, and nothing shall by any means hurt you.

The Workout

Luke 11:20

But if I cast out demons with the finger of God, surely the kingdom of God has come upon you.

Matthew 10:7-8

And as you go, preach, saying, "The kingdom of heaven is at hand." Heal the sick, cleanse the lepers, raise the dead, cast out demons. Freely you have received, freely give.

Conclusion: Jesus loves me and trusts me and, because of that, He has given me authority to cast out devils in His name. I speak with new tongues. No serpents or deadly drink can hurt me, and when I lay hands on the sick, they recover. I also raise the dead. I thank God and rejoice that my name is written in the Lamb's Book of Life.

ɛͻ

Luke 10:20

Nevertheless do not rejoice in this, that the spirits are subject to you, but rather rejoice because your names are written in heaven.

Revelation 13:8

All who dwell on the earth will worship him [the beast], whose names have not been written in the Book of Life of the Lamb slain from the foundation of the world.

Conclusion: Because the Lord loves me, my adversaries are broken to pieces, and the Lord thunders against them from Heaven. God gives me strength and exalts His power within me.

క్ర

1 Samuel 2:10

The adversaries of the LORD shall be broken in pieces;
From heaven He will thunder against them.
The LORD will judge the ends of the earth.
"He will give strength to His king,
And exalt the horn of His anointed."

Conclusion: God loves me and because He placed me in Christ, those who come against me are broken to pieces.

క్ర

Matthew 21:44

> *And whoever falls on this stone will be broken; but on whomever it falls, it will grind him to powder.*

Conclusion: Because of the love God has for me, He causes the enemy to be exposed and uprooted from the land by His power operating through me and has given me authority over ALL spirits in Jesus' name.

જી

John 3:20

> *For everyone practicing evil hates the light and does not come to the light, lest his deeds should be exposed.*

1 Corinthians 4:5

> *Therefore judge nothing before the time, until the Lord comes, who will both bring to light the hidden things of darkness and reveal the counsels of the hearts. Then each one's praise will come from God.*

Ephesians 5:11-13

And have no fellowship with the unfruitful works of darkness, but rather expose them. For it is shameful even to speak of those things which are done by them in secret. But all things that are exposed are made manifest by the light, for whatever makes manifest is light.

1 Thessalonians 5:5

You are all sons of light and sons of the day. We are not of the night nor of darkness.

Deuteronomy 11:24a

Every place on which the sole of your foot treads shall be yours.

Psalm 6:10

Let all my enemies be ashamed and greatly troubled;
Let them turn back and be ashamed suddenly.

Leviticus 26:7

You will chase your enemies, and they shall fall by the sword before you.

The Workout

Ephesians 6:17

> *And take the helmet of salvation, and the sword of the Spirit, which is the word of God;*

Conclusion: Because God loves me, my enemies fall before me by His Word that I speak.

ॐ

Revelation 19:10

> *And I fell at his feet to worship him. But he said to me, "See that you do not do that! I am your fellow servant, and of your brethren who have the testimony of Jesus. Worship God! For the testimony of Jesus is the spirit of prophecy."*

Conclusion: Because God loves me, He gives me a plentiful supply of the testimony of Jesus Christ, the Spirit of prophecy.

ॐ

Ephesians 2:4-6

> *But God, who is rich in mercy, because of His great love with which He loved us, even when we were dead in trespasses, made us alive together with Christ (by grace you have been saved), and*

raised us up together, and made us sit together in the heavenly places in Christ Jesus.

Exodus 4:11-12

So the LORD said to him, "Who has made man's mouth? Or who makes the mute, the deaf, the seeing, or the blind? Have not I, the LORD? Now therefore, go, and I will be with your mouth and teach you what you shall say."

Conclusion: Because God loves me, He has placed me in Christ on His throne at His Right hand, and I declare boldly His Word that He puts in my mouth.

৪০

Joel 2:30

And I will show wonders in the heavens and in the earth:
Blood and fire and pillars of smoke.

Conclusion: Because God loves me, when I speak, the Lord performs wonders in the heavens and the earth—blood and fire and pillars of smoke.

৪০

The Workout

1 Corinthians 3:17

If anyone defiles the temple of God, God will destroy him. For the temple of God is holy, which temple you are.

Psalm 50:3

Our God shall come, and shall not keep silent; A fire shall devour before Him, And it shall be very tempestuous all around Him.

Psalm 97:3

A fire goes before Him, And burns up His enemies round about.

Colossians 2:9

For in Him dwells all the fullness of the Godhead bodily;

Conclusion: Because God loves me, He lives within me, and He does not keep silent. A fire goes before me and burns up my adversaries.

ৎ

Psalm 18:14

He sent out His arrows and scattered the foe,
Lightnings in abundance, and He vanquished
them.

2 Samuel 22:14-15

The Lord thundered from heaven,
And the Most High uttered His voice.
He sent out arrows and scattered them;
Lightning bolts, and He vanquished them.

Conclusion: Because the Lord loves me and lives within me, He thunders from Heaven and utters His voice, sending out arrows and lightnings, running my enemies off.

જી

Romans 14:17

For the kingdom of God is not eating and drink-
ing, but righteousness and peace and joy in the
Holy Spirit.

Conclusion: Jesus loves me. He has given me righteousness, peace and joy in the Holy Ghost.

જી

The Workout

Psalm 104:4

Who makes His angels spirits,
His ministers a flame of fire.

Conclusion: God loves me and has made me His minister. I am His flame of fire.

ം

Zechariah 2:5

"For I," says the Lord, "will be a wall of fire all around her, and I will be the glory in her midst."

Conclusion: Because the Lord loves me, He is a wall of fire around me and the glory in the my midst.

ം

Psalm 5:11

But let all those rejoice who put their trust in You;
Let them ever shout for joy, because You defend them;
Let those also who love Your name
Be joyful in You.

Conclusion: I love the name of Jesus and rejoice and sing and shout for joy, and the Lord covers me with His presence and defends me.

ഗ

Zechariah 2:8

For thus says the LORD of hosts: "He sent Me after glory, to the nations which plunder you; for he who touches you touches the apple of His eye."

Conclusion: My heavenly Father loves me. He who touches me touches the apple of His eye.

ഗ

Galatians 5:14

For all the law is fulfilled in one word, even in this: "You shall love your neighbor as yourself."

Deuteronomy 28:9-10

The LORD will establish you as a holy people to Himself, just as He has sworn to you, if you keep the commandments of the LORD your God and walk in His ways. Then all peoples of the earth shall see that you are called by the name of the LORD, and they shall be afraid of you.

The Workout

Exodus 23:27-28

I will send My fear before you, I will cause confusion among all the people to whom you come, and will make all your enemies turn their backs to you. And I will send hornets before you, which shall drive out the Hivite, the Canaanite, and the Hittite from before you.

Conclusion: Because the Lord of Hosts loves me, He has made me part of a holy people who obey the commandment of the Law of love. The nations shall see that I am called by the name of the Lord, and they shall be afraid of me. My enemies shall be confused and full of fear. They will be destroyed as they run from my presence.

ℰℴ

Psalm 29:11

The LORD will give strength to His people;
The LORD will bless His people with peace.

Conclusion: The Lord loves me. He makes me strong and keeps me in peace.

ℰℴ

Isaiah 26:3-4

You will keep him in perfect peace,
Whose mind is stayed on You,
Because he trusts in You.
Trust in the LORD forever,
For in Yah, the LORD, is everlasting strength.

Conclusion: God loves me and I trust Him. That's why I have peace, and He gives me strength.

ະ

Romans 8:6

For to be carnally minded is death, but to be spiritually minded is life and peace.

Conclusion: God loves me and has given me the mind of the Spirit, which is life and peace.

ະ

Matthew 7:24

Therefore whoever hears these sayings of Mine, and does them, I will liken him to a wise man who built his house on the rock.

The Workout

James 1:23-24

For if anyone is a hearer of the word and not a doer, he is like a man observing his natural face in a mirror; for he observes himself, goes away, and immediately forgets what kind of man he was.

Romans 12:21

Do not be overcome by evil, but overcome evil with good.

Conclusion: Because the Lord loves me and I love Him, I easily overcome evil with good.

&

Hebrews 13:15

Therefore by Him let us continually offer the sacrifice of praise to God, that is, the fruit of our lips, giving thanks to His name.

Psalm 16:11

You will show me the path of life;
In Your presence is fullness of joy;
At Your right hand are pleasures forevermore.

Conclusion: I love God. I praise Him, thank Him, confess Him and glorify His name with my lips. God loves me and has put me on the path of life, where I receive the fullness of joy from His presence.

ଈଠ

Zechariah 2:10

"Sing and rejoice, O daughter of Zion! For behold, I am coming and I will dwell in your midst," says the LORD.

Conclusion: Because the Lord loves me and lives in me, I sing and rejoice!

ଈଠ

Isaiah 35:10

And the ransomed of the LORD shall return,
And come to Zion with singing,
With everlasting joy on their heads.
They shall obtain joy and gladness,
And sorrow and sighing shall flee away.

Conclusion: Because He loves me, God makes sorrow and sighing to flee away from me, and I sing with gladness and with His joy upon my head.

The Workout

Zephaniah 3:17

> *The LORD your God in your midst,*
> *The Mighty One, will save;*
> *He will rejoice over you with gladness,*
> *He will quiet you with His love,*
> *He will rejoice over you with singing."*

Conclusion: Because God loves me, He rejoices and sings over me too.

ॐ

Psalm 1:3

> *He shall be like a tree*
> *Planted by the rivers of water,*
> *That brings forth its fruit in its season,*
> *Whose leaf also shall not wither;*
> *And whatever he does shall prosper.*

3 John 1:2

> *Beloved, I pray that you may prosper in all things and be in health, just as your soul prospers.*

Conclusion: Because God loves me, it is His will that I prosper. So, I prosper.

ॐ

Philippians 4:19

> *And my God shall supply all your need according to His riches in glory by Christ Jesus.*

Conclusion: God loves me and supplies my needs through Christ Jesus, according to His riches.

ଈ

Ephesians 3:20

> *Now to Him who is able to do exceedingly abundantly above all that we ask or think, according to the power that works in us.*

Conclusion: God loves me and does exceedingly above what I ask or think by His power at work within me.

ଈ

Deuteronomy 28:1-8

> *Now it shall come to pass, if you diligently obey the voice of the LORD your God, to observe carefully all His commandments which I command you today, that the LORD your God will set you high above all nations of the earth. And all these blessings shall come upon you and overtake you, because you obey the voice of the LORD your God:*

The Workout

Blessed shall you be in the city, and blessed shall you be in the country.

Blessed shall be the fruit of your body, the produce of your ground and the increase of your herds, the increase of your cattle and the offspring of your flocks.

Blessed shall be your basket and your kneading bowl.

Blessed shall you be when you come in, and blessed shall you be when you go out.

The LORD will cause your enemies who rise against you to be defeated before your face; they shall come out against you one way and flee before you seven ways. The LORD will command the blessing on you in your storehouses and in all to which you set your hand, and He will bless you in the land which the LORD your God is giving you.

Conclusion: God loves me and, because I listen to and obey the voice of the Lord by observing the Law of love, I am set in Christ above all the nations of the earth. I am blessed in the city, the field and as I come and go; I'm blessed in the fruit of my body and of my ground, and I'm blessed in the fruit of my cattle and in the increase of my sheep; I'm blessed in my kitchen and in my bank account;

the Lord commands a blessing to my bank account which is my storehouse, and the Lord commands a blessing on all that I set my hand to do; my enemies are defeated to their faces and flee from me seven ways.

ഇ

John 14:13-14

And whatever you ask in My name, that I will do, that the Father may be glorified in the Son. If you ask anything in My name, I will do it.

Conclusion: Jesus loves me and that is why whatever I ask in His name, He does it, so that the Father is honored.

ഇ

Mark 11:23-24

For assuredly, I say to you, whoever says to this mountain, "Be removed and be cast into the sea," and does not doubt in his heart, but believes that those things he says will be done, he will have whatever he says.

Therefore I say to you, whatever things you ask when you pray, believe that you receive them, and you will have them.

The Workout

Conclusion: The Lord of Hosts loves me. Therefore I get what I say I'll get, because I believe it and know I have it.

ཚ

1 John 5:14-15

Now this is the confidence that we have in Him, that if we ask anything according to His will, He hears us. And if we know that He hears us, whatever we ask, we know that we have the petitions that we have asked of Him.

Conclusion: Because I know that the Father loves me and hears my prayers, I get the answers I'm expecting.

ཚ

John 15:7

If you abide in Me, and My words abide in you, you will ask what you desire, and it shall be done for you.

Conclusion: Because God loves me and has placed me in Christ, whatever I ask for is done for me.

ཚ

Philippians 4:6-7

> *Be anxious for nothing, but in everything by prayer and supplication, with thanksgiving, let your requests be made known to God; and the peace of God, which surpasses all understanding, will guard your hearts and minds through Christ Jesus.*

Conclusion: My heavenly Father loves me and that is why I pray with thanksgiving, letting Him know my requests. After that, I choose not to worry about the request anymore and, as a result, I'm peaceful inside

৪১

Matthew 19:26

> *But Jesus looked at them and said to them, "With men this is impossible, but with God all things are possible."*

Conclusion: God loves me. He is the God Who makes the impossible possible for me.

৪১

The Workout

2 Corinthians 1:20

For all the promises of God in Him are Yes, and in Him Amen, to the glory of God through us.

Conclusion: Because God loves me, all of His promises are Yes and Amen to me.

~

Romans 4:21

And being fully convinced that what He had promised He was also able to perform.

Psalm 119:89

Forever, O LORD, Your word is settled in heaven.

Conclusion: Because He loves me and I love and trust Him, I'm convinced that He does what He says He will do.

~

Psalm 89:7

God is greatly to be feared in the assembly of the saints,
And to be held in reverence by all those around Him.

Conclusion: God loves me. All the people shall greatly fear Him in the assembly of the saints, and those around will reverence Him.

೫

Psalm 22:27-31

All the ends of the world
Shall remember and turn to the Lord,
And all the families of the nations
Shall worship before You.
For the kingdom is the Lord's,
And He rules over the nations.
All the prosperous of the earth
Shall eat and worship;
All those who go down to the dust
Shall bow before Him,
Even he who cannot keep himself alive.
A posterity shall serve Him.
It will be recounted of the Lord *to the next generation,*
They will come and declare His righteousness
to a people who will be born,
That He has done this.

Conclusion: I love the Lord. All the inhabitants of the earth shall remember Him, and all the people shall bow down and worship Him as Ruler of the Nations. All those upon the earth shall bow before the Lord and tell of Him, declaring His righteousness to those not yet born, the truth of what the Lord Jesus Christ said from the cross: "IT IS FINISHED!"

છ

If you are a married man:

Proverbs 31:10-31

Who can find a virtuous wife?
For her worth is far above rubies.
The heart of her husband safely trusts her;
So he will have no lack of gain.
She does him good and not evil
All the days of her life.
She seeks wool and flax,
And willingly works with her hands.
She is like the merchant ships,
She brings her food from afar.
She also rises while it is yet night,
And provides food for her household,
And a portion for her maidservants.
She considers a field and buys it;
From her profits she plants a vineyard.

Bearing Fruit Without Ceasing

She girds herself with strength,
And strengthens her arms.
She perceives that her merchandise is good,
And her lamp does not go out by night.
She stretches out her hands to the distaff,
And her hand holds the spindle.
She extends her hand to the poor,
Yes, she reaches out her hands to the needy.
She is not afraid of snow for her household,
For all her household is clothed with scarlet.
She makes tapestry for herself;
Her clothing is fine linen and purple.
Her husband is known in the gates,
When he sits among the elders of the land.
She makes linen garments and sells them,
And supplies sashes for the merchants.
Strength and honor are her clothing;
She shall rejoice in time to come.
She opens her mouth with wisdom,
And on her tongue is the law of kindness.
She watches over the ways of her household,
And does not eat the bread of idleness.
Her children rise up and call her blessed;
Her husband also, and he praises her:
"Many daughters have done well,
But you excel them all."

The Workout

Charm is deceitful and beauty is passing,
But a woman who fears the Lord, she shall be
praised.
Give her of the fruit of her hands,
And let her own works praise her in the gates.

Conclusion: Because God loves me, He gave me a good wife. My wife is god-fearing, obedient, faithful and true to God and to me, desiring no other. She is loving, patient and kind to our children, disciplining them with patience and will never leave me.

ꝏ

If you have children or desire children (either natural or spiritual):

Psalm 127:3-5

Behold, children are a heritage from the Lord,
The fruit of the womb is a reward.
Like arrows in the hand of a warrior,
So are the children of one's youth.
Happy is the man who has his quiver full of them;
They shall not be ashamed,
But shall speak with their enemies in the gate.

Conclusion: Children are a heritage from the Lord. Because God loves me, He gives me many (spiritual) children.

೧

Psalm 128:3

> *Your wife shall be like a fruitful vine*
> *In the very heart of your house,*
> *Your children like olive plants*
> *All around your table.*

Conclusion: The Lord loves me. He makes my wife to be a fruitful vine and gives me children like olive plants around my table.

೧

Psalm 78:4-6

> *We will not hide them from their children,*
> *Telling to the generation to come the praises of*
> *the* LORD,
> *And His strength and His wonderful works*
> *that He has done.*
> *For He established a testimony in Jacob,*
> *And appointed a law in Israel,*
> *Which He commanded our fathers,*

The Workout

That they should make them known to their children;
That the generation to come might know them,
The children who would be born,
That they may arise and declare them to their children.

Ephesians 6:4

And you, fathers, do not provoke your children to wrath, but bring them up in the training and admonition of the Lord.

Conclusion: Because I love the Lord, I encourage my children by giving them instructions from the Bible and telling them of His strength and wonderful works.

৪৹

Psalm 103:17

But the mercy of the LORD is from everlasting to everlasting
On those who fear Him,
And His righteousness to children's children,

Proverbs 20:7

The righteous man walks in his integrity;
His children are blessed after him.

Psalm 115:13-15

He will bless those who fear the LORD,
Both small and great.
May the LORD give you increase more and more,
You and your children.
May you be blessed by the LORD,
Who made heaven and earth.

Conclusion: Because the Lord loves me and I love Him, my children are blessed with the presence of God in their lives.

৯০

Proverbs 14:26

In the fear of the LORD there is strong confidence,
And His children will have a place of refuge.

Psalm 91:9-11

Because you have made the LORD, who is my refuge,
Even the Most High, your dwelling place,
No evil shall befall you,
Nor shall any plague come near your dwelling;
For He shall give His angels charge over you,
To keep you in all your ways.

The Workout

Conclusion: The Lord is my Refuge. Because the Lord loves me and I walk in the reverential fear of the Lord, my children are protected and safe.

ଚ

Isaiah 54:13

>*All your children shall be taught by the LORD,*
>*And great shall be the peace of your children.*

Conclusion: Because the Lord loves me, He causes my children to be obedient to me and to Him, and they, therefore, have great peace.

ଚ

Psalm 72:4

>*He will bring justice to the poor of the people;*
>*He will save the children of the needy,*
>*And will break in pieces the oppressor.*

Acts 16:31

>*So they said, "Believe on the Lord Jesus Christ,*
>*and you will be saved, you and your household."*

Conclusion: The Lord loves me. Even if I am with Him in Heaven, my children will be saved, delivered and protected

As our Lord, JESUS CHRIST, said from the cross:

"IT IS FINISHED!"

Biblical Prayers

The tongue of the wise useth knowledge aright:
but the mouth of fools poureth out foolishness.
Proverbs 15:2

We should never use ritualistic prayers repeated over and over, if those prayers are not Holy Spirit breathed. Even prayer taken from the Scriptures will be of no effect except the Holy Spirit quicken His Word. Jesus taught:

But when ye pray, use not vain repetitions, as
the heathen do: for they think that they shall be
heard for their much speaking.   Matthew 6:7

The following prayers are only common-sense guidelines that come directly from the Bible. They are Holy Spirit-breathed prayers. When we pray in agreement with His Word, we are returning His

Word to Him. So, let's return the Word of God to Him today:

> *So shall my word be that goeth forth out of my mouth: it shall not return unto me void, but it shall accomplish that which I please, and it shall prosper in the thing whereto I sent it.*
>
> Isaiah 55:11

Don't forget that God is concerned about what concerns you. So, tell Him what concerns you and let it go into His hand. Then don't complain to Him about it anymore. Complaining isn't prayer that works. If you feel pressed to bring up something to God again, thank Him for the answer. Pray in faith, believing. And may God bless your understanding.

In the prayers that follow, please insert the appropriate term (me, I, myself, she, her, herself, he, him, himself, the name of the person, etc.)

The following prayer is based on 1 Corinthians 2:9-10 and Ephesians 1:17-21 (AMPC).

Heavenly Father.
In Jesus' name, I ask You to make _____ to realize and perceive what You have revealed by

Biblical Prayers

Your Spirit to my spirit. In order that _____ may be a blessing to others, I ask You to give _____ a spirit of wisdom and revelation of insight into mysteries and secrets in the deep and intimate knowledge of You and Your Word. And may the eyes of _____'s heart be flooded with light so that _____ could know and understand the hope to which You have called _____ and how rich is Your glorious inheritance in _____, and so that _____ could know and understand what is the immeasurable and unlimited and surpassing greatness of Your power in _____, as demonstrated in the working of Your mighty strength that You exerted when You raised Christ from the dead and seated Him at Your own right hand.

In the mighty name of the Lord Jesus Christ I pray,
Amen!

The following prayer is based on Proverbs 4:18 and 10:17 (AMPC).

Heavenly Father,
You said in Your Word that the memory of the righteous is blessed. Therefore, I ask

Bearing Fruit Without Ceasing

You to make _____ to remember all that
You reveal to _____ and that _____
also remember(s) the Scriptures _____
read. I also pray that You cause _____
to shine more brightly each day from the light
of Your presence within _____, as Your
Word finds place in _____.

In the mighty name
of the Lord Jesus Christ I pray,
Amen!

The following prayer is based on Romans 8:38-39
and Philippians 1:9-11 (AMPC).

Heavenly Father,
You said that neither death, nor life, nor angels, nor principalities, nor powers, nor things
present, nor things to come, nor height, nor
depth, nor any other creature shall be able to
separate _____ from Your love in Christ.
Therefore, I pray that _____'s love may
abound yet more and more and extend to its
fullest development in knowledge and all keen
insight in greater depth of acquaintance with
You and more comprehensive discernment, so
that _____ may truly learn to sense what is vi-

tal and approve and prize what is excellent and of real value, recognizing the highest and the best and distinguishing the moral differences, and that _____ be untainted and pure and unerring and blameless, so that with a sincere heart, firm in faith and spotless, _____ may approach the day of Christ, not stumbling nor causing others to stumble and that _____ abound in and am/is filled with the fruits of righteousness and of right standing with You and right doing, which come through Jesus, so that Your glory be both manifested and recognized in _____.

In the mighty name of the Lord Jesus Christ I pray, Amen!

The following prayer is based on Colossians 1:9-12 (AMPC)

Heavenly Father,
I ask that _____ be filled with the full deep and clear knowledge of Your will, in all spiritual wisdom and in comprehensive insight into Your ways and purposes and in understanding and discernment of spiritual things, and that _____

may walk, live and conduct _____ in a manner worthy of You, Lord, fully pleasing to You, and that _____ please You in all things, bearing all manner of the fruit of Your Spirit in every good work and steadily growing and increasing in and by the knowledge of You, with fuller, deeper and clearer insight, acquaintance with You and recognition of You, and that _____ am/is invigorated and strengthened with all power according to the might of Your glory, in order that _____ might, as necessary, exercise every kind of endurance and patience, perseverance and forbearance, with joy and with thanksgiving to You, for qualifying_____ to share the portion which is the inheritance for Your holy people, the saints in Light.

In the mighty name of the Lord Jesus Christ I pray, Amen!

The following prayer is based on 2 Thessalonians 1:11-12 (AMPC).

Heavenly Father,
I ask that You count _____ worthy of _____ calling and, in accordance with

what You have purposed to accomplish through _____. I ask that, by Your power, _____ may complete that work in faith, as _____ lean(s) on You in absolute trust and confidence in Your power, wisdom and goodness. May the name of the Lord Jesus Christ be glorified and become more glorious in and through _____, and may _____ be glorified in You, according to Your favor and blessing given through the Lord Jesus Christ to _____.

In the mighty name of the Lord Jesus Christ I pray, Amen!

The following prayer is based on 1 Thessalonians 3:12-13 (AMPC) and James 3:2 (AMPC).

Heavenly Father,

I ask that You make _____ to increase, excel and overflow in love for the brethren in Christ and all other people, in order that You may confirm and establish _____'s heart to be faultlessly pure and unblamable in holiness in Your sight, Father, and in the sight of the Lord Jesus Christ at His return. By Your

Spirit, Father, direct _____'s speech as _____ am/is yielded to You, in order that _____ don't/doesn't say the wrong things and in order that _____ has _____ character fully developed into the perfect man/woman, able to control _____'s whole body and curb _____'s entire nature into that which is well pleasing to You.

In the mighty name of the Lord Jesus Christ I pray, Amen!

The following prayer is based on Colossians 4:2-6 (AMPC) and Philemon 6 (AMPC).

Heavenly Father,
I ask that, by Your Spirit, You help _____ to be earnest, unwearied and steadfast in _____'s prayer life and that _____ (am/is/are) alert, giving thanks to You in prayer. As a result of Your powerful presence within and upon _____, Father, I pray that You open a door of utterance with boldness and doors of opportunity to proclaim the mystery of the Gospel by divine appointments, and that _____ may proclaim the

message fully and clearly. Father, by Your Spirit, help _____ to behave _____ wisely among the unbelievers, making the most of every opportunity, and may _____ know how _____ ought to answer every person. And I pray that the sharing of _____'s faith produces full recognition, appreciation, understanding and precise knowledge of all that belongs to every born-again believer in Christ.

In the mighty name
of the Lord Jesus Christ I pray,
Amen!

The following prayer is based on Proverbs 10:5, 10:17 and 11:30 (AMPC), 1 Peter 5:20 (AMPC) and Psalm 51: 6 (AMPC) and 51:12-15 (AMPC).

Heavenly Father,
I ask that You make _____ to be a wise <u>son/daughter</u> gathering in the harvest of souls for You. You already said in Your Word that the harvest is ripe. Make _____ to be a soulwin-ner. Make _____ to know truth in _____ inmost being, in order that _____ may walk in righteousness and be an example for all to see

the right path. By the abundance and overflow of Your Spirit within _____, let Your Spirit overwhelm those _____ walks by and those who come near to _____. Overwhelm them with Your presence, Lord, causing them to come to a true place of repentance and a time of decision. Thank You, Father, for causing them to be convicted of sin and convinced of the truth of Your Word and for making them ready to become born-again Christians. By Your Spirit, help _____ to capture human lives for You, as a fisher of men, women and children, saving them from the jaws of Hell and from the devil, who wishes to see the people burn in the lake of fire with him.

Use _____ to convert sinners, bringing them to you by Christ Jesus and saving them from death and destruction. Deliver _____ from bloodguiltiness, Lord. Don't let anyone's sin be on _____'s hands. May _____ speak faithfully to those to whom You send _____ and not bring shame to You by sleeping during harvest.

In the mighty name
of the Lord Jesus Christ I pray,
Amen!

Coming to Know Christ

We can all be trees of righteousness that bear fruit without ceasing if we will only take our Lord seriously. He is the Maker of the Universe, not an errand boy! He is the One Who put breath in you and me. After all has been said and done, it will be you, all alone, facing the Lord of Hosts.

At the judgment, none of us will be able to point to someone else and say it was that *"woman You gave me"* who is to blame. None of us will be able to point and say it was because of "that man You gave me." We will be unable to justify ourselves before the Lord with the excuse of "that preacher who fell" or "all the other people were doing it." No one, absolutely no one will be there to justify you … unless the Lord Jesus Christ Himself does it, and that will be impossible if you do not abide in Him.

I know it will bring sorrow to His heart and tears to His eyes, if any one of us fails to walk in obedience to Him, and He is forced to say, "Depart from Me! I never knew you." Therefore, let us endeavor to know Him.

> *And this is eternal life: [it means] to know (to perceive, recognize, become acquainted with, and understand) You, the only true and real God, and [likewise] to know Him, Jesus [as the] Christ (the Anointed One, the Messiah), Whom You have sent.*   John 17:3, AMPC

Salvation is not about how much you know *about* the Lord; it's about knowing Him personally. Going to Bible college can't save you. Being a pastor can't save you. Going to church can't save you. Even knowing the Bible can't save you. It is all about knowing Jesus and having a wonder-filled relationship with Him through the Holy Spirit. It is about being immersed in His love and delighting in Him through and in praise. It is about lining up the inside with the outside, as we walk out this wonderful salvation in obedience to His precepts.

Knowing the Lord is to know salvation, and you, too, can be a tree that bears fruit without ceasing!

Coming to Know Christ

The [uncompromisingly] righteous shall flourish like the palm tree [be long-lived, stately, upright, useful, and fruitful]; they shall grow like a cedar in Lebanon [majestic, stable, durable, and incorruptible]. Planted in the house of the LORD, they shall flourish in the courts of our God. [Growing in grace] they shall still bring forth fruit in old age; they shall be full of sap [of spiritual vitality] and [rich in the] verdure [of trust, love, and contentment]. [They are living memorials] to show that the LORD is upright and faithful to His promises; He is my Rock, and there is no unrighteousness in Him.

Psalm 92:12-15, AMPC

Here is my prayer for you:

Heavenly Father;
Thank You. Thank You for drawing those reading this prayer nearer and nearer to You, as You conform each one to be made into the image of our Lord Jesus Christ.
I thank You, Holy Spirit, for bringing the holy written Word of God to life, within and through those reading this. I thank You for bringing Your rain of refreshment upon their souls.

Bearing Fruit Without Ceasing

Have Your way, Oh God, in all the earth! Let the Word of God spring forth in righteousness within them! Use them to bring revival! Use them to bring revival to the nations! Use them to bring revival so powerfully that ALL confess that You are the only true God!

In the name above every name, the Lord Jesus Christ, we pray, Amen!

A Prophecy

Thus says the Lord, "If you will but hearken unto My voice, the voice of My holy written Word, being careful to humble yourself to it and to Me and be diligent to speak My Word in the appointed season, in what I set before you to do and to whom I send you, then I shall be with you and in you, quickening My Word. You and others shall see My glory, for I shall be upon you and the Word I send.

"All shall see that I AM God, and there is none beside Me, and every knee shall bow before Me. As you continue to abide in Me and I in you and run the race that is set before you, being diligent in it, I shall teach you how to run with a steady pace that spawns patience, that you may, patiently and without ceasing, bear an abundance of enduring fruit—fruit that remains."

"Behold, I come quickly!"

says the Lord.

My Purpose

The purpose of this book is to feed your spirit man in order to make you strong. Moreover, it is my desire to see men and women rise up in love, faith and obvious holiness, believing the Word of God and remaining continuously filled with the Holy Ghost, going about doing good and doing great exploits in the name above every name, Jesus the Christ, Who is Lord of all. May the Word of God be honored and magnified in the lives of all of us who name the name of Christ.

Reverend Steve Murr

AUTHOR CONTACT PAGE

You may contact Rev. Steven Murr in the following ways:

Mailing address in the U.S.
Rev. Steve Murr
c/o Barbara Howard
1901 Sheffield Ave Apt E6
Muscle Shoals, AL 35661-3143

Address in the Philippines
234 Aries St. Lot 4, Block 6
Riverside Sharina Heights St. Nino Apt. Taculing
Bacolod, Negros Occidental
Philippines   6100

Mobile number in the Philippines
(Globe): 011-63-9278531080

E-mail address
overflowing_glory@yahoo.com

Web address
http://usacominghome.wix.com/his-flag-ministries
https://www.facebook.com/ReverendSteveMurr

.